INTRODUCTION TO IGBO MYTHOLOGY FOR KIDS

INTRODUCTION TO IGBO MYTHOLOGY FOR KIDS

A FUN COLLECTION OF HEROES, CREATURES, GODS, AND GODDESSES IN WEST AFRICAN TRADITION

Chinelo Anyadiegwu

BLOOM BOOKS
FOR YOUNG READERS

Published by:
Bloom Books for Young Readers,
an imprint of Ulysses Press
PO Box 3440
Berkeley, CA 94703
www.ulyssespress.com

ISBN: 978-1-64604-314-9
Library of Congress Control Number: 2022936260

Printed in the United States
10 9 8 7 6 5 4 3 2 1

Acquisitions editor: Claire Sielaff
Managing editor: Claire Chun
Project editor: Renee Rutledge
Editor: Michele Anderson
Proofreader: Barbara Schultz
Front cover design: Jake Flaherty
Cover illustration: Jovilee Burton
Interior artwork: section start pages © ADELART/shutterstock.com
Production: Yesenia Garcia-Lopez

For my mother, Nkoli,
The Child of Story.

CONTENTS

Ndi Igbo Enwe Ézè

Igbo People Do Not Have Kings

INTRODUCTION

Igboland—Ala Igbo—is the ancestral land of Igbo people. It is in what is now southeastern Nigeria in West Africa. Its settlement precedes written history. Traditionally, Igbo society is structured around self-ruling communities connected by trade routes and separated by forests, lakes, and other natural barriers. In Igbo oral history, the first ancestor was Eri. Eri settled by the Omambala river around the ninth century, in what is now known as Aguleri.[1] Over time, his children traveled out to settle in different locations, and some descendants traveled to nearby tribes, often returning with new traditions. Ǹrì is the descendant of Eri, and the spiritual head of one of the oldest kingdoms in Igboland, Ọ́ràeze Ǹrị, the Kingdom of Nrì. The descendants of Eri contributed a lot to what is now considered standard Igbo culture, but there are many differing and sometimes contradictory traditions among Igbos.

The kingdom of Nrì has a spiritual head, called the Ézè Ǹrì, and his leadership came from his connection with Chineke,

---

1   Alice Apley, "Igbo-Ukwa (ca. 9th Century)," October 2001, https://www.metmuseum.org/toah/hd/igbo/hd_igbo.htm.

the creator spirit. A popular saying in Ala Igbo is "Igbo enwe ézè," or "Igbos do not have kings." Instead, what rules an Igbo person is the spirit, chi, that represents their destiny and the contract they made with the creator when that person was born. Igbo people answer to the piece of this spirit that rests in them, and to each other.

Igboland has numerous lineages, which can also be called clans. Igbo communities, and villages are largely made up of kin. Each has its own cache of stories, and the variety of origin myths reflects this abundance. One of the most popular stories—and my personal favorite—comes from UmuNrì (the children of Ǹrì). They came from the first ancestors, Eri and his wife, Namaku. Before the UmuNrì were made, the world was covered with water; then Chukwu, the great spirit, pulled up anthills from the ground and made dry land. He summoned Eri and Namaku from the sky and showed them the land. He taught them how to farm and told Eri to spread this knowledge throughout Igboland. Eri became the Ézè Ǹrì, the head priest, of what would be the Nrì kingdom.

That is just one story from one lineage. There are many other origin stories, because there are numerous Igbo clans, so much so that they can't be counted in full. Each community that settled an area has a different story that explains their community. For example, some tribes claim to be descended from the children of Eri and Namaku, while other tribes are believed to have migrated into Igboland from surrounding areas. Other origin stories describe the first people being made from the soil or from other deities. Despite all these different tales, Igbo communities have a lot in common.

Section I addresses some of those similarities and Igbo culture as I experience it. It also explains the general structure of the Igbo community and spirituality. Section II has stories. These sections are followed by a glossary.

The stories in this book are just one small part of Igbo culture—mine. I learned a lot of the information from my mother, grandfather, uncles, aunties, or cousins. I was told some stories while I was half asleep but pretending I was not. Others I begged to hear as I grew older. The ancestors of my people laughed and fought and loved. They made demands of gods and spirits. They lived and told stories about it all. We continue in their stead.

My name is Chinelolumu. I am a child of red soil and river pythons. Let me tell you about my people.

SECTION I
THE IGBO PEOPLE

CHAPTER 1
IGBO CULTURE

IGBO WORLD VIEW
(ỤWÀ NDỊ IGBO)

Igbo people understand the world (Ụwà) as having three realms: the sky (Igwe), the earth (Anị), and the spirit world (Mmụo). In the sky and on the earth is life, where humans and all visible things (plants and other animals too) live. Another world, the spirit world, is separated from but intimately connected to the visible world. The material, or physical, world affects the spirit world, and vice versa. Igbo reality doesn't fit into neat boxes of right and wrong, up and down. Instead, think of the world as two mirrors facing each other; the sky is one mirror, and the ocean is the other. The earth is between these reflections, like a doorway with infinity on both ends. A doorway is an entrance, but not an origin. It connects realities. The earth's position as a doorway allows it to serve as a connection between the sky and the ocean, but also the material and spiritual worlds.

This connection between the visible and spirit worlds also links life and death. Igbo people believe in reincarnation. When an Igbo person dies, that person returns to the spirit world and then comes back to the physical world in a new body. But this cycle of life, death, and life again does not last forever. A person who lives a virtuous life can become an honored ancestor, meaning that the person can stay in the spirit world, where a specific place is reserved for ancestors. There, these honored ancestors can live as they would in the physical world, except they do not die.

The sky is home to some of the core deities of Igboland. Chukwu, the great spirit, is said to hold meetings in his obi-ukwu (court). No human has seen Chukwu's court. Stories have it that Chukwu has an obi, a large meeting room, just like in a human compound. It is made from clouds instead of earth; plants that live on air grow in spiral designs around the obi's walls and across the bottom of the obi. What the spirits talk about is not for humans to know, and Igbo people do not directly concern themselves with the affairs of spirits. Instead, dibìàs and ézès are the intermediaries between the realms. More than anyone else, they understand the ways of the spirit realm. Alusị—deities—such as Amadịọha, Igwe, Anyanwụ, and Ọnwa, stay in the sky with Chukwu, although they have different realms (see Chapter 2). The earth, or ground, is home to Anị, the alusị that represents the earth. Her body holds land, water, humans, and other spirits. In her stomach lie all the dead and the living.

Chi is one of the most important concepts in Igboland. Chi translates as "spirit," but a person's chi represents more than that. Everything comes from Chukwu, including chi, so Chukwu has a say in everything. A person's chi is what was created first in that person. It holds their destiny, which they decided on with Chukwu when they were being created. The destiny agreed on between a person's chi and Chukwu is known only to the two of them. Igbo people traditionally believe that fulfillment is about discovering and fulfilling that destiny. An Igbo person's chi is reincarnated after death, while the physical body remains in the earth and returns to the elements. Each life in the cycle of reincarnation is meant to give a person a chance to attain the destiny predetermined by their chi and Chukwu. Therefore an Igbo person needs to connect with and understand their chi to achieve their goals. A common saying is that "if a person says yes, so does their chi"—or, in Igbo, "onye kwe, chi ya ekwe."

The Igbo word for human is m̀madù. Some people break down this word into two words, mma (goodness) and dù (is). Other people break it down into mma and ndù (life). Either way, being human in Igbo culture is about goodness and life. "Goodness" is defined by a person and their community, but honoring traditions and supporting your community are generally considered good. The aspiration for a good life, achievement within yourself and community, is the baseline of Igbo culture.

CALENDARS

This is the story of the Igbo calendar. Ézè Nrì, the head priest, was visited by four spirits—sometimes they were fishers or market sellers, the details change, but there are always four spirits—who told him what the days were and helped him organize the Igbo calendar. In Igboland, there are four days (ụbòsì) in a week (izù), seven weeks in a month (onwa), and thirteen months in a year (arò, àkà, or afo). There is an extra day at the end of every year dedicated to spirits.

The Igbo weekdays are Èke, Oyè, Àfò, and Ǹkwọ, and are named after the messenger spirits that visited Ézè Ǹrì. The days are also called "market days" because different communities pick one of the days to hold a market; therefore, a market is always open somewhere in Igboland. The spirits guard all the trade on their days. Communities have different spirits or stories tied to their markets. The spirits could be wise elders, beautiful youths, or lively children.

IGBO COMMUNITY

The Igbo community starts with the family. Traditionally, Igbo communities did not have rulers. Most communities were groups of large families and if they were governed at all, it was by priests, elders, and councils. Most often, a community or village shares a common patrilineage or matrilineage. Each family lived in a compound (ńbala), a walled, circular space with several small houses. The ground of the compound would be made up of packed red earth smoothed to accommodate humans. The center of the compound was an obi, where the head of the family lived and welcomed visitors. The rest of the family would live in different houses placed throughout the compound. Houses in Igboland are made from red earth and wood, bound together by woven cords, and their roofs are made of bundles of dried raffia. Each house has anywhere from two to four rooms, although wealthier compounds can easily have houses with double the usual number of rooms. Typically, the first room is public and the rooms in the back or at the sides are private, but Igbo houses do not follow a standard interior design. Compounds can have three-sided open sheds used to house yams and other crops. Sometimes crops can also be bundled with netting and hung from wooden support poles. A big harvest of yams is something to be proud of in Igboland. A compound also holds a family temple dedicated to an alusi̱. Elders and other adults in the family can have their own temples, and the head of the family usually has an ikenga, a physical representation, often carved from wood, of willpower.

The compound is the smallest unit of an Igbo community. Towns or villages are larger communities and extensions of the compound. Connecting towns or villages traditionally share lineage. All the communities together form the Igbo tribe as a whole. Often, communities are linked by meeting circles that grow bigger with each additional grouping. Igboland is a tapestry of interconnected communities separated by hills, forests, rivers, farmland, and other geographic features.

TITLES

In Igbo culture, to take a title is to take on a leadership role in your community. A title like ézè means priest and leader. This is because, traditionally, ézès were spiritual leaders as well.

Ézès can commune with spirits and guide the people through any issues that arise. An ézè can be consulted in times of war or famine, or about a marriage or birth. Ézès, however, do not dominate or dictate to people with their power; they support the people with their strength and wisdom. In fact, the kingdom of Nrì never had a standing army. Instead, priests, diviners, and crafters would try to solve the problems of the communities they visited through Igboland. They would be called in to settle disputes or perform a cleansing to wipe away great sins or to send away troubled or malicious spirits. Sometimes they would even visit a community with a message or demand from an alusị. The crafters would take on apprentices, teach skills, or sell their wares.

The most important aspect of a leader is their ability to serve. Some titles, such as Ọmụ, Nzè, and Ọzo, are earned with age and given to elders for their wisdom and service in the community. Other titles are given to people who achieve great things, such as hunting a leopard or growing huge quantities of food.

Titles like Òbi and Igwe are newer in Igboland. They were introduced by Igbo people returning from other lands. These titles are for leaders and, thus, such titles are the closest Igboland gets to having a ruling class. An Igwe or Òbi rules over a community that has a council of elders. They preside over meetings, and their word often carries the most weight in the community. At the same time, they aren't free to do as they please and are accountable to the same community they lead. In extreme situations, any leader can lose their title.

A dibìà is another category of title in Igboland. Dibìàs are healers, diviners, herbalists, and spiritual leaders. They do everything from making medicine to communicating with spirits. A dibìà is usually called into service for a spirit. The rites of initiation for different spirits are kept secret and known only to those who are called. A dibìà is sometimes called a dibìà afa or onye afa. "Afa" means "divination."

The Igbo people can give themselves a personal name in addition to their birth names. We can also acquire a title or a personal name from family and community members by doing brave or crafty things, or by having prominent character traits like being fast or funny or having a nice voice. A strong person might have the word agụ, meaning tiger, in their personal name. One of the names my mother calls me translates to "calm waters" because she says I can be calm on the surface, with a rush of current underneath. My teachers used to call me ọnụ, which means "mouth," because I talked a lot.

Igbo titles and personal ways work in different ways that can change from one community to another. For example, di means "husband." At the same time, di is also added to words to show that someone is the best at something in their community. Dimgba is a common title for the best wrestler in an age grade, or in a village. For a person to be a good wrestler, their spirit has to be one.

In Igbo reality, everything in the physical, material world is an expression of a spirit. This includes the things we do, so a funny person has a funny spirit. The name is an attempt at honoring and recognizing the spirit being shown. A name carries a spirit in that way. So when a person's spirit is strong enough to manifest in a way the community recognizes, it is fitting to give that spirit a name.

IGBO ART

I believe that we Igbo people, at our core, value connection. When you dance, you create a connection between your spirit, thoughts, and your body. When you tell a story, you create a connection between people. When you carve or make pottery, you create a connection between yourself and the earth. As with most things in Igboland, art is linked to the spirit. When you connect, you create something—life. Igbo culture honors and supports life.

MUSIC

Igbo people play music on many different occasions. Festivals, wrestling tournaments, title-taking ceremonies, births, deaths, and marriages are all causes for music. Music is also used to accompany stories. Igbo people use drums, flutes, gongs, and stringed instruments. Igbo instruments can be made from wood, clay pots, or metal. Larger drums can reach as high as an adult's knees or can be small enough to carry in one hand. One popular Igbo instrument is the ogene, a metal gong with two bell-shaped hollow parts. It looks like two cowbells that have been connected. Musicians use a wooden stick to play the ogene and make different rhythms. Besides the ogene, Igbo people also use instruments like ụbọ aka, a kind of thumb piano, or the "talking flute" ọja, which is used for many things, including wrestling competitions, dancing, and speeches. Igbo is a tonal language, which means the way something is pronounced affects its meaning. A skilled ọja player is able to imitate the tones of conversation, so much so that you can make out the words from the flute sounds! There are also simple instruments like an ajali, a shaker instrument made from calabash wrapped in string of beads. To use it, you just have to shake it to a rhythm. I have fond memories of growing up and running around with an ajali in hand.

ÙLÌ

Ùlì is a design style that uses dye or paint to re-create natural and symbolic patterns. Ùlì designs are used as decorations for important events and ùlì art can be found in, and on, houses of important people in a community. Ùlì is traditionally considered a women's design, because it came from Ani, the alusị of the earth. While primarily women create ùlì art, whether it is dyed into fabric or painted directly on the body, all genders wear ùlì designs on their bodies or fabric. Ùlì drawings are usually made from black and indigo dyes. Ùshe, which is similar to Ùlì, uses red dye. Spirals and circles are common shapes. Animals can also be part of the design: a tortoise can represent wisdom or trickery; the leopard is represented by its paw print; and the snake is depicted with curves or spirals. Some alusị, like Amadịọha, are also represented; his symbol is a five-peaked thunderbolt. The symbol for Anyanwụ—the sun—is a circle surrounded by lines emanating from but not touching the circle. Also, ùlì is used in paintings and murals.

CRAFTS

Igbo people are craftspeople, but our crafts focus on everyday things rather than grand sculptures. I think this occurs because of the way we view life. We find beauty in the things that we consider to be commonplace. Igbo crafts include clay pottery, metalwork, cloth weaving, and beading.

Mbari houses are a type of spiritual art in Igboland. They are made to honor Ani̇ and painted with ùlì. These houses use wood and earth like other Igbo buildings, but they are filled with carved figures representing other spirits and Ani̇'s family. The figure of Ani̇'s spouse, Amadi̇oha, with Ani̇ next to her, is in many mbari houses.[2] Mbari houses also include carved objects from daily life, such as pots and stools. When a mbari house is complete, it is closed off and left to naturally decompose back to the earth.

STORIES

Stories are an important part of Igbo culture. Moonlight tales (egwu onwa) are communal events where everyone gathers and trades stories or plays music. These stories were important ways to pass down Igbo culture, history, and tradition. Proverbs (inu or ilu) are also important parts of Igbo culture. My grandfather and my mother raised me with proverbs. I still do not understand some of them. I'll share one: "A new chicken moves with one leg." It means that you should be careful when you are in a new situation. The knowledge my

---

2   Amadi̇oha is sometimes referred to as Anyanwu̇'s partner, though this designation is rarer.

elders gave required a narrative I had to work to understand. This made it more effective and fun.

Many Igbo people are writers, storytellers, and musicians. In Igboland, a story is told with music, rhymes, and audience interruptions. The stories in this book include some of the more common ones, as well as a few that I have not heard outside my family or village. Igbo storytellers share common characters, themes, and sometimes, songs. What makes a story stand out is how well the teller can tell it. Some people are good at voices or music. Others add unexpected twists to the story. Peers tell stories to entertain each other, and elders tell stories to teach lessons or share their experience. Following my ancestors' lead, I used the differences between my stories and theirs to share my experiences and lessons I have learned, and to entertain.

GAMES

One of the most popular games in Igboland is nchò or ịchò; the full name is ǹchòlòkòtò. It is very similar to the two-person game of mancala, which is played throughout Africa and Asia. But nchò is indigenous to Igboland. It is played by placing small seeds or stones into different groups, also called houses, and trying to collect as many seeds as possible. The winner is whoever has the most seeds at the end of the game.

Wrestling (m̀gba) is also very common in Igboland. It can be played to gain a title, impress a future spouse, or just for fun. In Igboland, the point of wrestling is not to harm anyone but to display skill. You win a wrestling match by throwing, flipping, or pinning your opponent on their back or lifting them off both feet.

CROPS

Yams are one of the most important crops in Igboland. Igbo yams are different from potatoes. They are giant and can easily be the size of a forearm! One of the biggest festivals is the New Yam Festival, which marks the yam harvest. People gather to dance, wrestle, sing, and enjoy the harvest. Everyone shares food, because there is enough to go around. Yams can be boiled, roasted over a fire, and pounded and fried in oil. Often they are cooked with vegetables and meat to form a dense porridge.

My favorite meal in the world is pounded yam with ọha soup. Ọha means the leaves of the African redwood tree and the soup is seasoned with dried fish and meat. I also like to eat pounded yam with red stew—made from tomatoes—and okra soup. This combination is not traditional–in fact, people consider it an abomination against food–but I love it. A more common way to eat yams would be with egusi soup. Egusi soup is generally made from ground melon seeds, pumpkin leaves, and palm oil, and seasoned with meat.

Cocoyam is another important crop. Unlike large yams, a cocoyam is a small root vegetable around the size of someone's fist. In Igboland, cocoyams were traditionally farmed by women, whereas yams were farmed by men. Nowadays anyone can farm both crops.

The kola nut, a small reddish-brown nut that in rare cases is white, is the most important produce in Igboland. However, the kola nut is not eaten casually. There is an Igbo saying that "he who brings the kola brings life." The kola nut is the concentration of the Igbo love of life. It is used to start meetings and important events. It is also used to offer friendship and to connect with spirit. Kola connects all the realms, which is why it brings life. Kola tastes like a mix of a coffee bean, cashew nut, and cacao bean. It has a crunchy texture and tastes earthy and a little bitter. The process of eating kola is called "breaking kola" or "ikwa ọjị" in Igbo. This phrase describes the eldest person in the room speaking prayers and saying blessings before breaking apart the kola nut with a small knife. Breaking kola is usually done by men, but titled women can participate—as with most things in Igboland, there are often exceptions. The pieces are passed around to the visitors, sometimes with palm wine, the sap of palm trees.

Palm wine is a very important part of Igbo culture as well, and my village, Oba, is known for the sweetest palm wine in all of Igboland!

CHAPTER 2
THE ALUSỊ: DEITIES

Alusị in Igboland are spirits—sometimes called deities or gods—that represent core aspects of life or community. The better-known alusị are the spiritual body of powerful concepts like truth and love or physical entities as the sun, rivers, or the earth. Alusị can be represented by carvings, drawings, and temples, but all depictions are fluid and depend on how a person describes them. How an alusị is understood changes according to the community. Each community cultivates a relationship with an alusị (or more often, several). In farming communities, land and harvest spirits are stronger. In warlike communities, battle or war spirits are stronger. The physical description and personality of spirits can also change, again, depending on the community.

"Ṁmụo" refers to spirits in general, that is, spirits that are not alusị or chi, specifically. It refers to any being that does not have a permanent physical body in the human realm. Water spirits, forest spirits, wandering spirits, and even animal spirits are in this category. Innumerable spirits reflect every possible form of existence. Ṁmụo are mostly neutral, but they can be malevolent, or "ajo-ṁmụo," meaning "bad spirit." This could just be the nature of the spirits, or they could be a human that had lived a poor life and had been rejected from the reincarnation cycle. An Igbo saying "Chineke bu ṁmụo," which means the creator is a spirit, emphasizes the importance of spirit and its connection to Igbo identity. Chineke is a spirit and the ancestors are spirits. The personal chi is a spirit too, but is tied to a physical form to express itself.

The focus of the relationship between an Igbo person and a spirit is respect and understanding. If a person has a relationship with a spirit, but the spirit does not seem to be responding or doing their job, the person can break whatever they are using to represent that spirit and begin a new or different relationship. After all, Igbo enwe ézè: Igbos do not have kings.

CHUKWU

Chukwu is the creator spirit. It is also known as Chineke. Chukwu can be broken down into "Chi-Ukwu," which means "great spirit." Chineke breaks down into "Chi-na-eke," which is "the spirit that creates."

Chukwu usually does not have a temple or statues to represent it, because the spirit is everywhere. We are living in it! The most powerful connection to Chukwu is internal; it is a person's chi. Chukwu has no common depictions, but everything is a representation of it. The depth of the oceans, the height of the mountains, the hottest days, and the coldest nights—that's where Chukwu is. Everything possible represents the creator spirit.

Like everything else, alusị are created from Chukwu. Unlike Chukwu, however, they can have identifiable personalities that reflect the energies and realms that they control.

ANỊ

Anị is the spirit of the earth. Her name translates as "ground" in Igbo. She is also referred to as a goddess. Anị's realm is life and death. She oversees marriage, fertility, art, and the harvest, as well as death and the underworld. The laws of Igboland are known as òmenàànì, which means "it happened on Anị." Everything that happens on the ground is in the jurisdiction of Anị; thus, crimes are called nsọ Anị because they are taboo in the world of Anị. When someone commits nsọ, it affects the whole community; and if the crime is severe enough (like murder), entire groups and everyone would be held responsible and not just the person who committed the crime.

Anị is one of the core spirits of Igboland, but every community has a different relationship with her. Farmers and people who work with the soil have stronger relationships with Anị because she guides their harvest.

Anị is beautiful. She is said to have dark brown skin with red undertones, like the earth in Igboland. She wears her hair in various styles—sometimes in the elaborate braids of married women, or in the locs of water spirits' hair, or she wears it loose and framing her face. Her personality is as profound as life and death. Everything we do on this land affects her, and everything on earth from Chukwu comes through her, so we are subject to her laws out of respect and gratitude.

AMADỊỌHA

Amadịọha, the alusị of truth, justice, love, and peace, represents the will of the Igbo people. He is one of the sky gods, dwelling in the realm of Chukwu. He speaks with thunder and sends his will with lightning. Some Igbo people trace their origins to him. They say he made humans by throwing a thunderstone—a small rock that he sends down to announce his lightning—at a tree. His symbol is a white ram and an ọfọ staff, carved from the fallen branch of a tree of the same name. The staff represents truth and justice. His color is either red or white.

Amadịọha is even-tempered but angered by injustice. If Anị makes the laws, Amadịọha implements them. Amadịọha is often placed next to Anị, especially in mbari houses. In many communities they are depicted as married.

ANYANWỤ

Anyanwụ, the sun god, is the eye of Chukwu. She is his messenger in the daytime because her eyes cover the entire earth. In some communities, Anyanwụ is a male spirit. Anyanwụ is tall and slender. Her skin shines golden brown and her hair is plaited in a spiral. She lives in the realm of the sky, like Amadịọha, but she stays in the sun. Some people say her messenger is a white bird. If you want to send a message to Chukwu, Anyanwụ might be your fastest option. Sometimes Anyanwụ is paired with Amadiọha, but only rarely.

The priests of Nrì revere Anyanwụ, and before colonization, it was common for titled people of Nrì to have scarification marks made diagonally across their face, which represent her light rays.

M̀MỤO MMILI

"M̀mụo mmili" means "spirit of the water" or water spirit. Water spirits are important, and plentiful, which represents the role of water in Igboland. This broad category can include such well-known spirits as Idemili, which guards the river around my people's lands. There is even the more modern Mami Wata, the water mother, who is said to enchant, give gifts, and place curses with the same breath. Water brings life and nourishes the doorway between worlds. Water is reflective and illusory, so water spirits tend to have the same qualities. Because of water's key role, stories of water spirits are as numerous as there are villages. "The First Mermaid," a story in this book, talks about a few such spirits.

AGWU

Agwu is an interesting spirit. It governs divination, knowledge, medicine, and health. It is said to be the patron of dibìàs, so sometimes a dibìà is also called onye agwu. This spirit makes dibìàs who they are. If a dibìà rejects the call from agwu, then the agwu already in them can become uncontrolled and dangerous for the uninitiated dibìà. This happens because of the spirit in them. It needs to be nurtured and tended to.

Agwu is formless and is known more by its impact on people than by its physical depiction. "Agwu" is also a word for madness; when the agwu in someone is not tended to, that person can become disoriented, shifting between this world and the next, or become subject to the maladies that the agwu would otherwise hold at bay.

EKWENSU

Ekwensu is a war god. He is also known for his trickery and wisdom. As with the tortoise, it is often unclear where his morals lie, but he is never boring. In some communities, Ekwensu is also the name given to bad spirits who seek to torment people.

War is not permanent, so Ekwensu is a god who should be called on rarely. He carries so much power that it is easy to mishandle it.

Ekwensu is talked about or sculpted as a beast-like spirit with horns and large fangs. Perhaps because of this, missionaries and colonizers considered Ekwensu to be the devil. Ekwensu is not the devil because Igbo culture doesn't have that concept. Every diety is a part of Chukwu and is fulfilling their purpose.

ÌFÈJIỌKỤ

Ìfèjiọkụ is the spirit of yams! She is under the realm of Anị, but she is almost as well-known because of the popularity of yams. The New Yam Festival is celebrated in her honor, although other communities sometimes have other spirits present. Ìfèjiọkụ isn't a traditional spirit, and some communities might not classify her as an alusị.

She is represented by figurines that show her carrying a basket, or sometimes by three separate spirits, perhaps to depict the harvest cycle. She is stocky and sturdy, like the crop she represents.

IKENGA

An ikenga is a representative item. People of status use an ikenga to represent their chi and their will. The spirit in their ikenga holds the determination to succeed. The concentration of this will is meant to help draw and hold success.

Ikengas can be bought directly from carvers or in the market, but they must be blessed by a dibìà, who calls the spirit into them. However, if an ikenga is not successful, it is common for the person who owns it to smash it and get a new one.

An ikenga is usually a horned figure of a human or spirit. Sometimes impressions are made in the figurine to represent ancestors or animal symbols of strength. The right hand holds a symbol of power, weapon, or a work tool like a blacksmith's hammer or carving knife.

ÒGBANJE

Ògbanje are in between spirits. They come into this world again and again, but they struggle to stay for a long time, because ògbanje do not come from the human cycle of reincarnation. Some people say they come from "nowhere," but that is not the whole story. Ògbanje make contracts with a spirit or god strong enough to grant them passage into this world. The spirits promise them things, usually in exchange for something else. Ògbanje have a short life because sometimes that is part of the bargain they struck, or sometimes the spirits in charge of their lives want them back. Unlike the contract between chi and Chukwu, ògbanje do not always get a fair contract. Their iyi ùwà, an item that represents their contract, also calls them back. Some people say that destroying an iyi ùwà keeps an ògbanje spirit in this realm. If the iyi ùwà is destroyed, however, their contract is destroyed too, and the ògbanje might never get what they came to this world to achieve. That would harm them and defeat the purpose of their journey.

Ògbanje take a lot of risks to come to this realm, and as with most Igbo people, ògbanje have a love for life. They want to do something; sometimes only they know what that is, but they will work to achieve it.

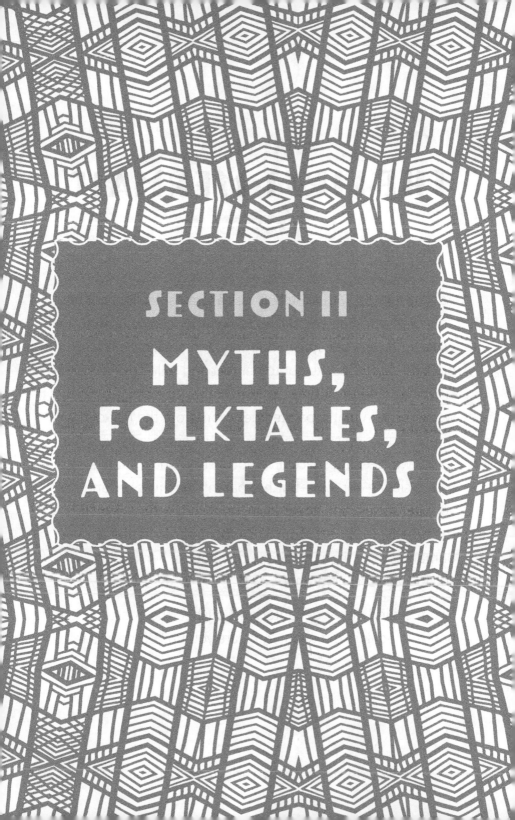

SECTION II
MYTHS, FOLKTALES, AND LEGENDS

CHAPTER 3
THE FIRST MERMAID

Adaku woke up with an itch. It was a familiar feeling, but tiny ants' feet prickling her skin was not the ideal sensation to wake with. She sat up, shuddering, and shaking the feeling out of her arms. Adaku got to her feet and rolled up her raffia sleeping mat just in time for her mother to swing aside the woven curtain that separated her room from the rest of their house. Adaku was the only one in her age grade who had their own sleeping space. Everyone else had to share space with a sibling—or four—but her parents had just her and her younger sibling, and he was too young to sleep by himself. By the time he needed a room, she would be living on her own, or married. The thought jolted Adaku out of her musings and she focused on her mother.

Nkem smiled at her daughter and pushed the basket in her hands in Adaku's direction. "Ada, are you up? Come and take your basket. Let's go."

Adaku quickly greeted her mother. "Enh, Mommy, good morning. I just woke up." She grinned and then averted her eyes. "Let me freshen up quickly. Then I'll join you outside."

Her mother laughed and shook her head. "But if I told you to go to the river now, you would be ready even before the rooster crowed." She turned to leave the room, saying the last few words as the curtain fell behind her. "Okay, I will wait for you outside."

Adaku stared at the curtain for a moment, then she rolled up her sleeping mat and put it away in the corner of her room with her other belongings. She looked through a small cloth bag, pulled out her chewing stick, and headed out of her room. Her younger sibling Kaira, waddled out of the room he shared with their parents and gave his sister a big grin while stretching out both hands. Her father followed behind him and scooped him up, causing Kaira to erupt in a fit of giggles.

"Nnànnà ka anyi ga kpata nkụ (Let's go and fetch firewood)." Keeping a firm hold on the giggling boy, he swung him over his shoulders. Kaira stretched his hands, and his fingertips just touched the wooden beams of their ceiling. Adaku's father walked toward his daughter and rested a hand on her head. "Did you sleep well, Ada?"

Adaku nodded and hugged her father before following him outside. Her mother, Nkem, was outside the house in deep conversation with Chizoba, her elder sister. Seeing the trio come out, they stopped talking, and Chizoba waved her hand in greeting, addressing Adaku's father first.

"Ugonna, good morning, you're going to get firewood? Bring us some too, oh." She patted Nkem on the back and turned to walk back toward her house on the other side of the compound.

Adaku had a bad feeling about their exchange, but she focused on getting ready. The sooner she could go to the market, the sooner she could leave. At that thought, the tingling under her skin got stronger, and Adaku rubbed her hands against her skin, not that it did much. This was not a physical itch. Adaku headed to the small clay washbasin at the side of her house and cleaned up. She filled up her water gourd, stuck her chewing stick in her mouth, and headed over to her mother.

Nkem already had two baskets of yams and cocoyams lined up. She gave Adaku a piece of patterned fabric—one of two short wrappers—that Adaku rolled up into a flat spiral and placed on her head. Nkem did the same, and they each picked up a basket and set off.

Kaira called out behind them. "Mommy, Adaku, bye-bye. Bring something from the market for me!" They laughed and did not respond, but Adaku was already thinking of what she could bring back.

Nkem and Adaku made their way through their community in silence. To get to the market, they had to leave the gathering of compounds that housed their immediate and extended family and make their way to the center, where the four neighboring communities met. They did not meet a lot of people on the way. The long journey meant most people set out before Anyanwụ, the sun goddess, first opened her eyes, but the sun's rays were already blanching the sky in veins of red and orange. Thanks to Adaku's late rise, they would be among the last ones to arrive. Adaku felt a twinge of guilt with every step, and she opened her mouth to apologize: "Mummy …"

"Ada, don't worry about it. The sun rises when it does, and the moon comes out in its own time too. You're a part of this world, so you have your own time as well. There's no point being something you're not."

Adaku went quiet, thinking about what her mother said. She wanted to believe that even her failures were part of who she was meant to be, but her life had everything except a plan. Everyone else in her age grade was preparing for who they were going to be, and she was lost. So, unless "lost" was who she was meant to be, Adaku felt like she was failing. Nkem let her daughter think in silence. The two of them walked off the cleared daily path and started on the outer, less traveled path. As they neared the market, they started to hear the hum of voices. Before long, they met the last group of people from the neighboring communities, and they made their way to the market together. Adaku stared at the family in front of them, a mother and her two daughters—well, she was actually looking at their goat. As it walked, it dropped small pellets behind it, and Adaku was forced to do a short, clumsy sidestep to avoid them. She heard a short laugh and she looked up to see her mother disappearing a smile. Groaning, Adaku moved sideways in an attempt to avoid the goat the rest of the way.

The Àfò market was crowded. People stood or sat on patterned cloth mats, with woven baskets full of crops. A few open fires, with metal pots covered by iron grills, were being tended to.

Some people were roasting yams, others corn or ube. A few people were even selling abacha. Adaku felt her stomach grumble at the sight of the cool white strips of cassava sitting in small bowls of water. Nkem must have heard it too because she responded.

"Let us settle down first, then you can go and get us something to eat, eh?"

Adaku nodded and hurried her mother away from the goat and its pellets and toward the nearest free space. The sooner they set up, the sooner she would have food. Her stomach grumbled again in agreement. The two of them set down their baskets and laid out their mats. Nkem bent to move her basket over to the mats, and then she caught sight of Adaku almost vibrating from eagerness. Nkem laughed and pulled out her money cloth, then she handed Adaku a few cowry shells. Adaku wasted no time and ran straight for the woman selling roasted yams. She returned to her mother, smiling and holding a bundle of roasted yams in banana leaves.

Nkem and Adaku spent the rest of the morning exchanging their produce for things they did not grow, like rice, and by the time the sun was at the midway point in the sky, they were out of yams and instead had an assortment of food, soap, and even a new, long piece of cloth. Adaku did not forget to get something for Kaira. She and Nkem traded a small piece of copper wire for a wooden nchò game set from a young apprentice carver eager to show them his creation. Adaku could already see the look on Kaira's face when she showed him the game.

The market was still busy: even more people had come with their animals, precious stones, clothing, and produce, but Nkem and Adaku were done for the day. As they started packing their things, Nkem sighed and began to speak.

"Ada, your aunty and I had a conversation earlier today. I want to talk to you about it."

Adaku felt the hairs on the back of her neck stand up. She clenched and released the muscles in her legs and wrists instead of doing what she felt the urge to do—run. She took a breath and let her mother continue. "What did you talk about?"

"You know your uncle, your father's cousin? He's a fisherman and he and his wives need more help, and so they can apprentice you to learn how to make fishnets. You would be by the river all the time. What do you think, nné? If not that one, Ejike's family is still proposing a marriage."

Nkem laughed and finished packing up the rest of their purchases. Their baskets were filled with entirely new goods. "You don't have to get married now, but if you want to have your marriage settled, you have that option. I want to know what you want."

Adaku listened to her mother while frowning. It was not that she did not want to be a fisher or that she did not want to marry Ejike. She felt neutral about these things, but she wanted something more than neutral, something life changing.

"I don't know what I want or why I have to want anything at all." She looked around at the familiar scene, even though it had some unfamiliar faces. This was all she knew—this market, her family. Why did anything have to change?

Nkem looked at her daughter, and she crouched down to her height and put her hands on her shoulders. "Ada, don't let me hear you say you want nothing, okay?" She kissed her daughter on the forehead. "You were brought here with a purpose. Even if your head doesn't know what it wants, your chi does. Your spirit does. So, when you're lost, or confused, or scared, always look to spirit, okay? You cannot want nothing, because you're not nothing. If this isn't it, we'll find something, eh? Calm your heart."

Adaku nodded, but she did not meet her mother's gaze. She let her mother pull her into a hug, and she took a deep breath. Maybe everything was going to be okay. They separated, Nkem picked up her basket, and Adaku bought some corn and ube before they left the market and started down the path back to their home. Every few steps, Adaku would open her mouth to say something, rethink it, and then continue walking. Nkem watched her daughter do this a few times before she prompted her to talk.

"Do you want to say something?"

Adaku nodded and responded, "I know we have so much to do when we get home, but can I go to the river?" She focused on the red earth at her feet.

Nkem nodded. "It has been awhile, hasn't it? Don't worry about dinner. Take some clothes with you and wash them while you're there. Come back before the sun starts to hide again. You need to see clearly to make your way back."

Adaku grinned and quickened her steps the rest of the way home. When they walked into the compound, Kaira was wrestling with one of his cousins, Zoba, while some of his other cousins cheered them both on from outside their wrestling circle. Once he noticed Adaku, he squirmed out of Zoba's grasp and, ignoring the opinions and calls from the crowd to return, ran to his sister.

"You're back! What did you bring for me?"

Adaku considered saying "nothing," but she could not stand to see the heartbroken look on his face. "I did get you something. Follow me inside. Let's drop these things first, and I'll give it to you." Adaku took the basket from her mother, and she and her brother went into their family home to drop off their wares. Once they got inside, Adaku sank down to the cool earth of the floor and started to pull out things. Before she could get to Kaira's present, her brother had already pulled out the small, wooden carved game.

"You got me nchò!" Kaira grabbed the game and held it over his head, shouting, "Thank you!" as he ran out the door to show his gift to his friends. Adaku laughed and finished putting up the rest of the wares; then she got their basket of clothes and started walking to the river near their compound. Before she got to the river, she could smell the water and the earth. To Adaku, river earth did not smell like land earth. It was almost like freshly tilled soil, but in addition to smelling like worms and bugs, it smelled like air. And fish. She laughed to herself.

No one else in her compound seemed to notice the river, not its smell or the many creatures that lived in it and by it. Besides commenting on the muddy riverbed, most people focused on each other. The river was where they gathered. For Adaku, the river was everything. It was the only thing that could calm the itch. All her life, Adaku had felt irritated by almost everything, except she was not *really* irritated. She was happy, but there was always an extra feeling, like being pulled. The feeling did not go away so she started calling it an itch. The only thing that could calm it was the river. Regular water did not work, and still water from the river did not work either. She had to find flowing water, dip her feet in it, and breathe in the air. The constant itch sometimes made her feel like screaming, and this was her only release.

The river was not crowded. Besides Adaku, there were three other people talking by the river: Chizoba's husband, Uzo, and two other men from nearby compounds. They noticed her and waved in greeting. Her uncle Uzo called out to her.

"Ada anyi you're here? You didn't go to the market with your mother today?"

Adaku nodded her head and walked toward the river, settling close enough to the men to hear them talk but far enough to wash her clothes without disturbing them.

"I went, but I wanted to come to the river, so my mother gave me these clothes to wash." She looked up at the sun, now far past the midway point, but the light had not started to dim. "I don't know if I'll be able to wash, since the sun isn't as hot anymore. It might be better to try again tomorrow."

The men laughed and one of them, the man in the middle holding a gourd of palm wine in one hand and a cane in the other, tapped his walking stick on the ground in amusement. "See how grown you sound?" He laughed. "I remember when we first welcomed you to this world. Now you're almost ready to manage your own household." His friends laughed, and the man to his right, Chizoba's husband, cleared his throat to speak, with laughter still in his eyes.

"Akaosa, leave her alone. What do you mean 'manage a household'? Before she does that, she must, of course, learn a trade first." He looked at Adaku and smiled. "What do you think, Ada? Your mother's sister told your mother about our arrangement this morning. Do you want to learn a trade? After all, you're always coming here."

Adaku looked at the water. "I'm thinking about it, Uncle, thank you."

Uzo frowned. "Ada, is there a problem?"

Adaku shook her head, "No, Uncle, there's no problem." Then, contradicting herself, she continued, "It's just that I don't know if learning a trade is what I want to do. I don't know if I want to do anything." She picked up a small stone from the ground beside her and tossed it into the river. "Everything is changing, but I don't want to change. I want to be me."

Uzo raised his eyebrows with new understanding. "Ada, everything changes, and everything stays the same. What matters is your choice. It's good that you want to be yourself. Keep doing that, and when the choices come, take the one that feels like you. You hear?"

He patted her on the back, and he and his friends stood up to go, while Adaku tried to keep herself from falling into the river from the force of her uncle's pats. The third man, who had been silent while they talked, moved toward her and helped her balance.

"Uzo, before you start giving advice, make sure the person you're advising can be alive to receive it, eh?" He smiled at Adaku before turning to leave with the others, their laughter echoing behind them. Adaku stayed at the river until darkness started to creep into the sky. She carried her basket of unwashed laundry and made her way home. She did not notice the small bubbles that rose in the water and how they moved through it with purpose.

When she got home, she joined the rest of her compound by the cooking fire outside their house. Kaira was dunking akpu, small handfuls of molded cassava paste into his soup, so quickly it looked like one continuous motion. He was swallowing it so fast that Adaku could not make out the soup he was eating it with. Adaku shook her head before she sat on a stool next to her mother and explained that she did not think the clothes would have a chance to dry. Smiling, she volunteered to go to the river again the next day.

"You don't need a reason to go back, but you can take the clothes again," was all Nkem said before handing Adaku a bowl of what she now recognized, from the bright green leaves, as ọha soup. Adaku washed her hands and followed her brother's actions, eating almost as quickly as she could breathe.

"Is that my daughter?" Ugonna's voice came from behind her, and Adaku did not get to turn before she felt her father settle on the ground beside her. "The last time I saw you, the sun wasn't even in the sky yet." He paused, noticing how quickly Adaku and Kaira were eating, and he shook his head. "Slowly, slowly, the food will not run away."

A few of her relatives chuckled, while Chizoba added, "It's not today that they started eating like this. Blame your wife for her cooking." Adaku and Kaira looked at each other, and then moved their heads away from their bowls and, with great difficulty, tried eating their food in smaller bites. Their actions caused another round of chuckles from their relatives. The people in the compound spent the evening talking until the darkness of night forced them to retreat to their sleeping areas.

The days passed. Adaku still was not sure what she was going to do, but her family had not stopped providing her with options. Each time she had to say she had not found her choice, Adaku wondered if she ever would. She tried to talk to her cousins about it, but she felt like they did not really understand.

"I don't see what the problem is," her cousin, Uju, said. "You're the prettiest person in all the neighboring communities. Who would not marry you? If you don't want to marry one person, marry another. It's not a problem, right?"

"Or you could not marry at all!" her younger cousin, Ifeoma, added. "You could just learn something, anything you wanted."

Adaku knew what she *could* do. The problem was that she did not know what she wanted to do, but no one else seemed to have that problem. Another big market day came and went, and Adaku still did not have any idea what she wanted her future to be. The next morning, she woke up expecting the same frustrating sense of confusion and longing, except it was not there. The first thing Adaku noticed was that the itch was gone, and the second was the silence. Her house was unusually empty.

Curiosity replaced confusion and Adaku walked outside to investigate. She did not have to move far because her answer was in the middle of her compound. Surrounded by almost all her family stood five of the most interesting-looking people Adaku had ever seen. Her family turned to look at her, drawn by the sound of her footsteps. For some reason, the strangers looked at her too. She greeted her family, tried to avoid the gaze of the strangers, and moved to stand by her mother. She wanted to ask what was going on, but anticipating her question, Nkem shook her head, indicating now was not the time. Adaku turned her gaze back to the strangers. They were still looking at her. Some of them looked happy, almost excited. The others just looked interested but not overwhelmed. Ugonna cleared his throat, and as one, the strangers turned to look at him.

"Who are your people?" Ugonna asked.

The stranger in the middle stepped forward to answer. He was tall and fair. Like that of most of his companions, his hair fell in tight locs, but he held his hair up with braids of coral. He had a short wrapper called an ogodo tied around his waist and between his legs. Strings of mollusk shells wrapped around his ankles. When he spoke, his voice was like a bubbling spring.

"My name is Ari." Then he pointed to his companions one by one, starting from his left. "That is Okpo, Awo, Iyi, and Asa." We come from a land across eight rivers. We traveled far to come here for one reason. Each of us would like to marry your daughter."

In the silence that followed, Adaku wondered if she could run back to her room and pretend she had not heard him. One of the strangers, Asa, seemed to have guessed Adaku's thoughts, and she smiled. Her side teeth seemed to be filed into short points. Adaku thought her smile felt like a dare.

"Adaku can barely handle one marriage, I don't think she can do five." Nkem laughed, but there was a hint of something Adaku didn't recognize under her voice and in the tightness of her eyes.

"No." This time Iyi spoke. Their voice sounded like the crashing of waves on a shore. "She can choose one of us, if she wants."

Ugonna started talking before Adaku could send them away. "Well, we don't know who you are, or where you came from. We can't just let you take our child. You can stay with us." He paused. "Usually, some of you would stay with Ada, but given the circumstances …"

"They can stay with me!" Chizoba volunteered. "I can find out everything. Don't worry."

"I wasn't worried." Ugonna said, but Chizoba was not listening. She gathered up the startled visitors and guided them to her own compound. Stunned, Adaku watched them go. What was happening?

Ugonna and Nkem left Kaira to play with other children and ushered Adaku back into their shared living space. They sat down to talk.

"Ada, do you know those people?" was the first thing Ugonna said.

"If I do, I've forgotten them. I don't think I've seen them before."

"Should we send them away?" Nkem asked, and Adaku heard what was under her voice clearer. Her mother was worried.

Ugonna shook his head. "No, if they're dangerous, I want to know who they are. If they aren't dangerous, having them stay won't matter." He paused. "Of course, Ada, if you want them to go, they will be gone tomorrow."

Adaku smiled. "Thank you. I think I'll go and see them later. I want to know how they know me too." More than that, the moment Chizoba left with the visitors, the itch had come back. Adaku now knew that they had something to do with that feeling, and she wanted to know what. Once she was done talking to her parents, she ran to Chizoba's compound. Her aunt greeted her with a knowing smile.

"Go and wait in the obi, I will bring them to you."

Adaku did as she was told, and shortly after, her aunt walked in with the visitors.

"I'll wait outside," she said, surprising Ada, and left the room.

Adaku stared at the strangers. They sat across from each other in silence until she broke it.

"Why me? What do you want from me? How do you know me?"

Okpo answered. His voice was deeper than the voices of the rest of them. He was lean, and he moved with a grace that was almost catlike.

"We don't know you. We were curious, because you called to us from so far away."

"What do you mean?"

Asa answered for him. "He means we're spirits, water spirits."

"Asa!" Ari seemed frustrated. He turned to Adaku.

"Sorry, that was not how I wanted to let you know."

"There's no point hiding it," Asa muttered. "We are from completely different worlds. It's better she knows."

"You're spirits?" Adaku's heart started racing. "Does that have anything to do with, I mean, am I like you? Is that why you've come?"

"You're nothing like us." Asa said. "Don't worry about that."

"What Asa means is—you're not a water spirit." Awo spoke last, and his voice was calm and measured, with little fluctuation.

Adaku looked at them again after getting this new information. It made sense. They were a little too beautiful, too perfect. Take Iyi, for instance. All the spirits had skin as smooth as pottery clay, but Iyi's was different. Their skin was almost too smooth, it seemed like it could melt and loose structure at any point. Adaku thought of Asa's pointed teeth and how all their voices sounded like water. Spirits. They were spirits. Spirits were trying to marry her. What?

"Okay, you're spirits. What do you want with me?"

"The five of us come from the same tribe," Ari said. "Our job is to guard one of the gates between this world and the spirit world. A new gate opened, and all five of us are eligible to be guardians, so we decided that whoever found the best partner would be the guardian."

"Then we felt your pull," Iyi continued. "We thought—who could be a better partner than a human who could call spirits, without even trying? We heard of your river visits from the small spirits that share the water with you. Every time you visit, they're drawn by the force of your desire. Something about you is special, even though we're not sure what."

"So you don't actually like me, you just want to win? So you can become some sort of guardian?"

"Yes," Asa said, at the same time the others cried, "No, not at all!"

Adaku frowned, "Asa, if you don't want to do this, why are you here?"

"I want to win, and I have to put up with this to do that. You are not going to choose any of us. We're spirits. We guard the gates from the spirit side. If you left, we don't know when you could come back. So, this whole thing is a waste. We shouldn't have come here, and we can use something else to determine who will guard the gate. You belong here, not in our world. Tell them that so we can leave."

Adaku hesitated. "What if I did want to go with you?"

"What?" all five spirits asked together, but Asa's voice was the loudest.

"For as long as I've been alive, I've felt this pull to water." Adaku kept her voice low as she talked. Besides her parents, she had not talked to anyone else about this. And even with them, it was only briefly.

Okpo agreed. "Yes, you call the water to you, and it calls back. We feel it too. We're not sure why."

"It hurts." Adaku said. "The first few days it's okay. It feels like an itch, but after a week? A month? It hurts. I feel like I'm dying of thirst, even if I drink water, it does nothing. I need..." Her voice trailed off.

"Living water," Asa finished the sentence for her. Asa's voice was softer than the last time she spoke. It was tinted with something that felt like empathy, but Adaku was not sure.

"Yes. Or you. I mean, all of you, apparently. It goes away when I'm around you." Adaku laughed nervously. "I'm not saying I'll marry you, but can I go back with you? Maybe if I stay with you long enough, the itch will go away."

"Maybe," Ari said, but he did not sound convinced.

"Well, I think it's a great idea," Iyi said with a grin. "The gates stay open for four weeks more, in your time. We were going to stay here for a few days before heading back. You can come with us and make your decision there. If you don't choose any of us, you can return home."

Adaku smiled. "Will I be able to find my way back?"

Awo answered with certainty. "Easily. The road we take is not a human one. If you don't come with us to any of our realms at the end of the journey, you will be right back where you started."

Adaku left the group and ran back to tell her parents what she found out. They listened to everything she said, including her request to go, before they spoke.

Nkem started. "When you were a child, you fell in the water. You were under for so long, we thought we lost you, but..."

Ugonna finished. "The water brought you back."

Adaku was shocked. She had never heard this story before.

Nkem apologized. "We're sorry Ada. I'm sorry. We should have told you, especially after you told us about the pull you feel."

"Almost losing you scared us. When you told us about the pull, it was like we were going to lose you again. The water had brought you back. Maybe it was calling for you again. We could not stand the thought." Ugonna had tears in his eyes when he talked. "We did not think about what it felt like for you." He dropped his head, and his wife picked up where he couldn't continue.

"Ada, we want you to have a good life, a full one, even after we leave this world." Nkem sighed. "We cannot keep you for ourselves. If you want to go on this journey, we support you."

Ugonna nodded as his wife talked. His emotions clogged up his voice, and he could not speak, but he stared at his daughter with all the love he could convey. Adaku hugged her parents.

The next few days were filled with preparation. Ugonna and Nkem asked the spirits every question they could think of, while Adaku spent all the time she could with her family. Kaira was the hardest person to say good-bye to. He ran away when she told him she was leaving, and when it was time to leave, he pulled on her leg, asking her not to go.

Asa stared at him for a moment before she broke the strings on one of the bracelets she wore. She pulled out a seashell and handed it to Kaira. "If your sister comes to our world, take this with you to the river, and you can speak to her."

Kaira let go of Adaku, clutched the shell firmly in both hands, and nodded. He would never lose it.

After Kaira let go, Adaku said good-bye to her family one last time. Besides the spirits, everyone was crying, even Adaku. Then she walked with them into the forest where the path to the spirit realm lay.

When the group left the sight of her family, the gravity of her decision sank in. She might not see her family for a very long time. Then again, she thought, how different would it be from going to a different town to fish or marry? At least this would be an adventure. Plus, she was not planning to marry the spirits anyway. Eventually they stopped at a puddle of water just wide enough for two bodies to pass through.

"It's here," Awo said. "There's no going back after we go through. You have to walk the entire path, even if you do not come to our realms with us. The spirit world can be dangerous. Are you sure?"

"If I wasn't, I wouldn't have come this far."

Awo nodded. "Good, then hold Iyi's hand. We'll go in one at a time. Ari and I will go first. Then you and Iyi. Asa and Okpo will come in last."

Adaku watched the two spirits jump into the puddle, and then she followed suit. The world around her twisted, and she landed on the sky. Wait, *on* the sky? Adaku looked around her. Somehow she was standing on a cloud surface, and the sky above her was soil. The only reason she was not screaming was that the spirits were acting as if everything were fine. They were surrounded by mist, so much so that their view faded into a dense gray fog not more than eight steps away from them. Beyond that, Adaku could see shadowy forms moving through the mist.

"It's strange, right?" Iyi said. They stood next to Adaku and mirrored her, looking at the topsy-turvy world around them.

Before Adaku could respond, Asa interjected, "We don't have time to talk. Let's go."

She started walking forward, and the others followed.

Adaku's journey through the spirit world was tense. The sky-ground made her nervous, and every so often, a face shaped from clouds would float away and hover next to her. The spirits said these faces were harmless, but they startled

Adaku every time they appeared. The hardest thing, though, was that Asa seemed to get angrier with her as time passed. Finally, Adaku walked up to her and asked for an explanation.

"Why are you so angry with me all the time? What did I do?"

Asa looked startled, and then she frowned. "You shouldn't be here."

"Why not? I was made from the water just like you!" Adaku had told them what her parents had said.

When she told them, Awo had nodded and said, "You were given life from water, like us. I understand why you call water. It's in you."

Asa shook her head. "No, you are not like us at all; we guard the gates. We were made to guard the gates. You, you are human, you just have a bit of something else, and that can make it hard in your world, but you'll survive. You do not have to come with us. You have a family and a life. Why would you change that?"

"First, I do not know if I am leaving with any of you or not, and second, if you know I am having a hard time, why don't you try empathy instead of judging me? Or you could leave me alone!" Adaku walked to the back of the line, choosing to stay next to Iyi. The spirit looked between her and Asa and chuckled but did not say anything.

They continued walking for longer—Adaku did not know how long—before all the spirits stopped. Adaku almost ran into Okpo's back before she caught herself.

"I am first this time," Awo said, and then he turned to look at Ada. "I have to go. Will you come with me?" Even as he asked, he sounded like he already knew the answer.

"I thought you came from the same place." Adaku said instead.

"We come from the same tribe, but we live in different waters," Okpo explained.

Adaku shook her head. "I'm sorry, I won't. But I am glad I met you." Awo smiled and stepped through a puddle of water that suddenly appeared in the clouds. "Maybe we will meet in another life," he said. Then he was gone.

The journey grew quieter. Over time, Adaku bonded with her companions, and now she considered them friends, but she might never see them again.

She jumped in surprise when Asa walked up to her, interrupting her thoughts.

"Sorry. I was not trying to scare you." She actually sounded apologetic.

"What do you want?" Adaku replied.

"To apologize. I mean it. You're right. I should be more understanding. It's just hard when you're jealous."

"Jealous of what?" Adaku's response was incredulous. "You're surrounded by people who know who you are and love you. For you. What else is there?"

Asa was slow to respond. She furrowed her brows and thought in silence while they walked, before answering. "The spirit world, my world, isn't like yours." She looked around. I mean, you see from this bit of it. It's nothing and everything all at once. It just is. I just got here and I'm already complete. I already know who I am, so that's how I'll be. But humans? You can create whatever you want. It doesn't matter what you've been or what you're expected to be. You can name yourself whatever you want, and you get to become that. If you're wrong, you can just come back and do it over again. I just am, you know?" She gestures at herself. "I've always been me. Nothing else."

"So, you're jealous because people get to lie to themselves?"

Asa's eyes widened in surprise at Adaku's question. "I never thought about it like that. With you, for instance, you get to be anything you want—a carver, a weaver, a leader. I thought you had something I really wanted: choice. Real choice, and it seemed like you were throwing it away." She paused, then her voice took on a hint of wonder as she continued. "I guess if you're here it can't have been that great, huh?"

"No, no you are right. My family is amazing. My life is amazing." She stopped talking and looked down. "Which makes it even worse that I'm not satisfied."

"Oh."

"Yes, everything just seems not enough, but I know it should be. Everyone in my family is working so hard for me to have all these options, but I don't want any of it. " Adaku changed the subject. "Is that why you don't want me to come with you? You think my life is better in the human world?"

Asa laughed, but she answered the question. "Spirits, we do a lot of watching. We see a lot of life, and yet we can have none of our own." Asa clutched the air. "I want more."

Adaku nodded. "I know the feeling."

Asa looked at her. "Yes, I think you do." Then she smiled, and Adaku felt her heart lurch.

She stuttered an excuse and ended the conversation, choosing to walk alone. From then, every time she looked at Asa, her heart would feel weird.

"Oh no."

Iyi was the next spirit to leave. Knowing it was their turn, Iyi raised an eyebrow at Adaku, who shook her head. They smiled and stepped into their gate, waving good-bye to Adaku. The last thing she saw was their smile. Adaku felt glum after Iyi's departure. She liked the water spirit, and now they were gone.

After Iyi left, Adaku stopped avoiding Asa and went back to talk to her. They traded stories. Asa told her about spirits, and Adaku shared stories of her life. Everything about her home delighted Asa, and her smiles became more frequent. Every time she smiled or laughed, the feeling in Adaku's heart grew stronger, but she did not stop sharing. She could not bring herself to do it. After Iyi was Okpo, then Awo. Each time a spirit left, they asked Adaku to come with them, and she said no. Then it was just her and Asa left.

"You really didn't go with them," Asa said, suddenly. "I should have believed you when you said you weren't sure if you were coming."

Adaku shook her head. "No, you shouldn't have." At Asa's confused look, Adaku hesitated, and then she decided to ask the question she could not bring herself to ask until now. "When you say you do not want me to stay is that because you don't like me? Would it ever be possible for you to like me?"

Asa stopped moving. She stood still for so long that Adaku thought she was frozen. Then she said, "You cannot ask me that. You should not be asking me that."

"What do you mean?"

"It doesn't matter what I want, Adaku. You do not belong here."

Asa looked her in the eyes and Adaku saw traces of fear, confusion, and... hope?

"I think I belong with you, more than I've ever belonged anywhere else. But if you don't feel the same way, then I'm wrong. What do you want, Asa?"

The spirit broke off their gaze and looked away. "You should go back. I'll be leaving soon."

"I don't want to go back if I cannot go with you."

"I'm a fish. We are water spirits, not humans. Don't you understand that? You will be miserable in the spirit world."

Asa's gate showed up, a small puddle like the others, and Adaku knew she did not have much time left.

"I won't be miserable if I'm with you." Adaku took the spirit's hand. "Asa, I'm going to ask you again. What do you want? What do you choose?"

Asa stared at the hands in hers, and she decided to be honest. She could do that if it was just the two of them.

"I want you to come with me. I'm sorry."

"Why would you be sorry about that?" Adaku said, laughing. "I'm telling you that I want to come with you!"

"It's selfish. You deserve more."

"You are more. This is more. Okay? I'm coming with you."

Asa remained silent before she nodded. "Okay, okay, yes. Yes. Come with me."

Adaku laughed and pulled her toward the gate. When they started to walk together, they both began to change. The queen of the water spirits had seen their bond, so she melded their spirits together, creating something entirely new. Their lower halves transformed into colorful tails. Adaku's tail was shaped like a fish's, Asa's was shaped like a snake. Adaku kept her human upper half, while scales covered most of Asa's back and arms. Her fingers had webbed skin between them, connecting them. They laughed when they noticed their change and without hesitation went through the open gate. Together they guarded the water realm, and Adaku became the first mermaid, transformed to reflect her love.

CHAPTER 4
THE TORTOISE AND THE BIRDS

The animal kingdom was experiencing a famine. The antelope and the deer grew lean from the browning grass. In turn, hunters like the leopard grew thin from the lack of prey. The animals gathered what they could. Some built nests or dug caves—making hiding spots of all sorts. Others fed and stored fat in their bodies for later. The python even went deep into sleep, planning to wake only when the earth was bountiful again. It was a time of rest and survival for everyone except Mbeku, the tortoise.

While the other animals suffered from the difficult times, Mbeku noticed that the birds stayed the same. Their feathers were still as fluffed, and while the other animals started to show bones through their skin, the birds grew healthier and more robust. Mbeku ran out of the food he had stockpiled and decided to approach the cuckoo bird. This red-chested cuckoo was known for being proud, and Mbeku knew just how to talk to him.

"I've noticed that your feathers still shine as they did before the famine!" Mbeku shouted from beneath the tree that Mara, the cuckoo, stood on. His words caused the bird to nod and pace back and forth on the branches, sometimes hopping to another branch.

"Of course they do," Mara said, and the bird flew down to stand on Mbeku's shell. "This famine belongs to the land, but in Igwe's realm, there is always food." Mara laughed and started to fly away, but Mbeku interrupted.

"Could you bring some food back for me?"

Mara shook his head and fluffed his wings.

"I wish I could, but I have no way to do that. I can't bring food from Igwe to Ani, but even if I was allowed to, I would not be able to carry anything." He spread out his wings to show his point.

Mbeku dropped his head. "I have no food and no great hunting ability like the other animals. I don't know if I will survive this famine."

Mara tried to cheer him up. "Igwe will send rain soon, and Ani will bring us food. Soon. It will be okay."

Mbeku did not respond, and in the silence, Mara got an idea.

"Wait!" Mara started to hop around Mbeku's shell in excitement, eventually flying to the front of the tortoise. "I have a plan!" Mara was too excited to notice the smile on Mbeku's face.

"What kind of plan?" Mbeku asked. By this point, the bird had abandoned all attempts at keeping still and was making small circular swoops in the air above Mbeku.

"I can ask the other birds for help! Come back here tomorrow before Anyanwụ rises!" was all Mara said before zooming off.

Mbeku let the bird get out of sight before he lifted his head. He did not hide the pleased look on his face, and he made his way back to his home. That night he had no food, but he slept well, thinking of the food that awaited him once he woke up.

The next day, Mbeku made it to the tree where he had met Mara, but the bird had not arrived yet. Mbeku paced as fast as a tortoise could pace, and before long, a line of flying birds graced the sky, with rays of light coming behind them. Mara had arrived, and he had not come alone.

When the birds landed, they took turns introducing themselves. Then, Mara explained what was happening. After leaving Mbeku the day before, he returned and asked Igwe to bless his wings so that he could share his ability to fly with Mbeku. Igwe told Mara that Igwe's decision had to be supported by the other birds, so if a flock of birds agreed to share their ability with Mbeku, then Igwe would grant the request. Mara beseeched the birds, and eventually he gathered enough support, and Igwe granted his request. After Mara finished speaking, each of the birds, one by one, gave Mbeku a feather. With the help of the birds, Mbeku climbed the nearest tree and unfurled his new wings. The birds flapped their wings, generating wind next to him, and Mbeku leaped. Instead of falling, he glided in sync with the rest of the flock. From below, they made a strange sight. The birds made the same triangular pattern they always did, but in the middle was Mbeku, slightly out of formation. The birds guided Mbeku to Igwe's realm, and they landed at the feast room.

Mbeku had not seen so much food since the famine started, and he could feel his stomach grumble. He started walking toward the food in a daze, but the birds stopped him.

"We have to wait for Igwe to tell us to eat." Mara explained. "The food is replenished every day, and we each take turns gathering food." Mbeku pondered what Mara told him, and then with a sly grin, he asked, "Whom is the food for?"

Mara smiled. "It's for all of us, of course."

The birds and Mbeku waited for Igwe's signal in comfortable silence. Finally, a voice, light yet dense as clouds, filled the room.

"Welcome. This feast is for all of you."

Mbeku felt soft, mistlike droplets of water on his skin, but he could see no water. It felt like he had plunged into thick fog, but he could still see. Igwe's voice sounded again, but this time it felt like the sound came from inside him, though he was sure the voice reverberated through the room as well.

"What is your name?"

The tortoise hesitated, and then he began to speak. "Ever since I was a child, my mother named me Unu, because she knew I would become wise to the world." Mbeku heard Mara's feathers ruffle at the fake name, but his friend didn't interrupt. Whether it was to help Mbeku pretend his name was "all of you" or because Mara was scared, Mbeku didn't know. He was grateful for the birds' silence all the same.

The tortoise felt the mist get thicker in the silence, and the air grew thin around him. He could not breathe for a moment, and then the pressure disappeared as if it had never been there.

"Do as you decide."

Igwe's presence left the hall, and Mara poked the tortoise with his feathered head.

"As our guest, you should go first."

The moment Mara gave him permission, Mbeku headed for the food. To the astonishment of the birds, Mbeku started eating and did not stop. By the time they regained enough control over themselves to ask him to stop, half the food was gone, with barely enough for everyone else to get scraps. The tortoise turned around to a row of angry birds.

"I can explain."

The birds did not say anything in response. They stared at Mbeku. Some of them fluffed their feathers, seeming to grow almost double their size in a moment. Mbeku started to withdraw his neck into his shell. This was getting bad.

Mara broke the tense silence.

"You betrayed us."

Mbeku poked his head out and shook it in response.

"No, no. I was only eating my share."

The birds did not seem convinced. They started toward the tortoise. Mbeku spoke in a rush, not stopping for breath.

"No, see, Igwe said, Igwe said it was for all of you. Remember, I said my name is Unu? Ununcha, that's 'all of you,' right? I just thought the food was for me. It was an honest mistake!"

Mara scoffed, and the rest of the birds tittered at his excuse. Their laughter came out in short clicks and whistles.

"You're still lying." Mara said. He did not sound angry; instead, his voice was hard and neutral. Mbeku started to think— maybe he had made a mistake. The birds reached the tortoise and formed a half circle around him.

"Return what is ours," Mara said.

"What do you mean—?"

The tortoise did not get a chance to finish his question before the first bird, a pied crow, pulled her feather away from the tortoise with her beak and then turned her back on him.

"No, wait. Stop!" Mbeku protested and tried to dodge as the birds enacted an alternate version of their actions earlier that day—they took back their feathers. Soon there was only a single feather left on Mbeku. Mara sighed and walked up to the tortoise, shaking his head. He took the last feather, and the birds opened up the circle for the tortoise to leave.

Mbeku looked around him in dismay. "I can't leave like this. I don't know how to get back down."

This time the eagle responded.

"You arrived with our support, but you forgot that once it was time to share. You don't belong here."

Mara added, "You don't make the choices you need to make to be here. We can't trust you."

The birds split the leftovers evenly between them and flew out of the feast room together. Mbeku was left alone. He walked to the edge of the entrance and looked down to see how high he was. He could barely make out the small flecks of what he realized were trees. Mbeku gulped. He closed his eyes and walked off the edge. As he fell, he tucked in his head and feet and hoped for the best. He felt the wind rush past him, and he heard the noises of surprise from creatures beneath him as he came into view. He laughed to himself as he imagined what he looked like—a headless shell—hurtling down from the skies. He poked his head out slightly, but the sight of the earth rushing toward him made him pull his head back in fright. The next thing he felt was the impact, and the last thing he heard was a shattering sound. Before he could register pain, he passed out.

When Mbeku came to, his view was blocked by a crowd of faces. Rather than looking concerned, the other animals looked at him with faces full of contempt.

"He's awake" he heard someone say. Then he felt something slow and slimy crawl onto his head. Two eyes poked down from above him, and the snail waved in greeting.

"Mbeku! What have you gotten up to again?" The snail, Eju, crawled down to the ground in front of the tortoise, and the other animals gave way. "Well, I did the best I could. How do you feel?"

The tortoise frowned and ignored the hostility of the crowd. "What do you mean, Eju?"

"Ah, well..." The snail looked uncomfortable, but he continued. "Your shell broke, eh, cracked a bit." Seeing the shocked look on Mbeku's face, he hurriedly continued, "It's okay. I mean, you're scarred, but you're okay. I honestly don't know what else you expected, jumping from the sky like that. You could have waited for the birds to cool off, you know."

Mbeku swung his head around to look at the top of his shell. What was once smooth and even now had uneven cracks throughout. He made small movements with his body and realized that, besides the scarring, he was okay. Mbeku looked at his back in silence and then turned to face Eju again.

"Eju, thank you. I don't know how I would have survived without your help."

The snail nodded. "Of course."

Mbeku continued speaking. "But how did you know about the birds?"

Eju took a look at the animals behind him, and then he dropped his voice and moved closer to Mbeku.

"The birds told everyone what you did. Some are angry that you broke your word like that. Others are angry that you planned to feast with no regard for anyone else on land."

Mbeku was annoyed. He raised his voice to address the gathered animals. "Say what you want about me being deceitful. That matter has been resolved. The birds took their feathers back. I realize that I made a mistake."

"A mistake?" The gazelle huffed and kicked his feet.

Mbeku noticed a few birds in the crowd, and they flapped their wings and clicked their beaks in rebuttal.

"Yes, a mistake," Mbeku continued. "But beyond that I did nothing wrong! I did not have a way to carry food back."

The parrot squawked. "If you had shared, you could have brought some food back for the others each time!"

"Nchokwu!" Mbeku yelled. "You're always starting trouble."

The parrot, Nchokwu, turned his head to the side and did not look at Mbeku. "I think you are the troublemaker between the both of us."

The animals laughed and Mbeku did not have a response. Frowning, he thanked the snail once more and made his way from the crowd. He had to go home. When Mbeku arrived at his small cave, he found the leopard stretched out across the entrance. He stopped moving.

"Um, did you need something from me?" Mbeku was thinking fast. He did not understand what he could have done to provoke such a mighty predator.

The leopard stood and stretched, and then she turned to face Mbeku. Her voice came out in low rumbles, "I won't share space with someone as selfish as you." She leaned back onto her hind legs and snarled. "Be grateful I'm not making a meal of you. Leave."

Mbeku nodded once, twice, three times and turned around. He did not care about the cave. Alive was better than anything. He would find shelter.

The next few days proved him wrong. Every time Mbeku found a place to settle down, the neighboring animals would tell him to leave. It seemed the birds had spread news of his actions across the land. Eventually, a small river snake came up to the tortoise.

"Mbeku, try going to the riverbank. You can take shelter in the water and come out to find sustenance." The snake did not stay for a response and slithered away.

Mbeku did as he was told. He chose a river to shelter by, and when he got there, he was pleased to find river grass growing in sparse clumps. It would not keep him happy, but he would survive. Mbeku spent four, eight, and then twelve days living by the riverbank. The crickets and small animals that lived nearby did not send him away. They did not seem to notice him at all. Mbeku watched one full moon pass, and then another. Every so often, he would venture out to check the temperaments of the other animals, but no one had forgiven him yet.

One day, Mbeku woke up to a silent riverbank, the kind of silence that appears only when a predator is nearby. He slipped into the water without causing much of a ripple and poked his head out to see if he could find out who was nearby.

It did not take long. A leopard prowled the riverbed and once Mbeku's eyes landed on her, she spotted him. Mbeku dipped his head back into the water, but it was too late. He could hear the leopard getting closer, or maybe that was his heart beating louder.

Then the water around Mbeku started to swirl. A gentle, amused voice filled his head.

"Mbeku, when will you learn? Fine. I will help you this time."

The tortoise felt his body begin to change. The ends of his feet flattened out into finlike points, his tail lengthened, and his heartbeat began to slow down. Mbeku was interrupted from taking stock of what was happening as a shadow covered the sky above him. He did not bother to look up. Mbeku took advantage of his new body and dived deep into the river. It felt as if the river were pulling him down and away from the riverbank. With his new flippers, Mbeku moved faster through the water than land. He felt a splash behind him and knew the leopard was coming after him. He kicked faster and followed the river, planning to keep going until it met the sea. The leopard kept behind him until the riverbed grew too far from the shore. Defeated, she growled once and swam away.

Mbeku did not stop moving. He would come up for air, but with his newfound skills, he did not need to stay by land often, and the water held plenty of food for him. He stayed like this for a few more moons. Mbeku had resigned himself to his new life when, with no warning, it rained. As if the dry spell had never existed, the rain continued to fall. The parched ground soaked up all the water. The trees grew lush and produced large bounties. The animals grew fat and healthy as the moons passed.

Eventually, the tortoise ventured out on land one day, and he discovered that the anger of the other animals had calmed. With food in their belly, they had warmth in their heart. The land animals offered forgiveness and permitted Mbeku to live with them again. Because of their forgiveness, the tortoise felt the magic of the river goddess revert, and he returned to living on land. However, the magic never fully left. Much later, Mbeku found that his descendants were born with patterns on their shells like he had, and some were born with flippers like the ones he had once had. From then on, some of his descendants would live on the land, while others would live on the water.

CHAPTER 5
THE WRESTLER WHOSE BACK NEVER TOUCHED THE GROUND

The entire population of Diobu was gathered in the square, or so it seemed. It was the last day of the Igu Aro festival that marked the beginning of the planting season and foretold the fate of the year to come, and the annual wrestling competition was taking place. The day before, the diviner had announced that the year ahead would be fruitful, so the people were ready to celebrate the good news.

The usually crowded market was cleared out. A circle was dug in the ground and filled with soft sand. This was where the wrestling would take place.

The people sat or stood around the circle, talking excitedly. A flute player sat on a stool at the front of the crowd. He brought his flute to his lips and started playing, prompting the two boys who had moved toward the center of the circle to approach each other. They were both bare chested, with short wrappers tied securely around their loincloths. One boy was visibly older. He was a head taller and already had signs of a beard. His body was muscular but agile. The other boy was barefaced but just as muscular. He smiled at the older boy.

Ikenna, the younger boy, stretched out his fingers and inhaled. He had just aged into a new wrestling grade, and this was his first match. He knew that no one expected him to win and just putting up a good match would preserve his honor, but he could not squash his desire to win.

The two boys clasped hands and then walked to opposite areas of the circle. Mirroring each other's movements, they squatted, held their arms out, and circled each other. Suddenly the older boy, Zimuzo, lunged at Ikenna.

Ikenna jerked his head back and dug his toes into the sand. He grasped the hand that came toward him and twisted his body in an attempt to flip the other boy. Ikenna's body bent back as a result, and he tightened his core to keep his balance. He kept pulling and tried to flip the older boy but Zimuzo grunted and pulled his body backward, his larger frame allowing him to resist Ikenna's pulling. Ikenna used the counterforce to pull himself back up, and then he backed away from Zimuzo's reach. Their first collision had ended in a draw.

The flute player upped his tempo, and the boys felt their hearts race to match it. They reached out at the same time and ended up in a grapple. Both boys squatted and pushed away from each other, teetering as they broke free. Ikenna dropped to his knees, and Zimuzo landed on all fours. Ikenna sprung up, and Zimuzo followed a moment later, which made all the difference. While Zimuzo was trying to stand, Ikenna grasped Zimuzo's left arm with both hands and twisted to the right. Zimuzo was still unsteady, so he could not withstand the force. His body flipped and he landed squarely on his back.

Ikenna raised his arms and the crowd cheered. Then he helped up Zimuzo, and the two grinned at each other.

"You're already stronger than me, eh, Ikenna? Take it easy. It's like you're trying to win it all."

Ikenna did not respond—he just smiled at the other boy before they both walked out of the ring. Ikenna waited by the side of the ring while other competitors fought. Soon it would be his turn again.

His next opponent was a tall, lanky boy named Ejike. No one was surprised that Ikenna won; this time much easier than the last. At the start, Ejike stretched out both hands to grab him, and Ikenna ducked, grabbed at Ejike's thighs, and then pulled. He was surprised at how well it worked. Ejike could not steady himself and he fell to the ground.

Ikenna won his next match too. His opponent this time was Lota, another boy about his age. Lota's previous match had been long and drawn out, while Ikenna's was the opposite. Even though Lota was skilled, Ikenna was moving more quickly and with more strength. Soon Lota met the same fate as the others who had faced Ikenna. There was one left.

The crowd cheered with increasing enthusiasm each time Ikenna won, and by the time the last round came around, their excitement had built so much that Ikenna thought he could see the tension in the air.

When Ikenna saw his last opponent, he knew it was going to be a difficult fight. It was midday, and the beads of sweat running down Ikenna's forehead stung at his eyes. Through his squinting, he could make out a boy who was at least twice his size. Ikenna was not even sure they should be in the same age grade.

Ikenna stood and stretched, and then he and his opponent met in the middle of the circle. From the chanting crowd, Ikenna learned that his opponent's name was Tochi. They clasped hands and separated. Ikenna squatted and dug his palms into the sand to dry off his sweat. He and Tochi circled each other, neither making the first move. Then Ikenna darted forward, and when Tochi moved to grab him, Ikenna shifted to his side. He was hoping that the larger boy would lose his balance, but Tochi recovered by taking steps forward to match Ikenna's momentum. Ikenna wrapped his arms around Tochi and tried to lift his opponent up but he would not budge. Tochi copied Ikenna's grapple, tightening his arms around Ikenna before bending forward to flip Ikenna, but the younger boy let go before his feet could leave the ground. They backed up and circled each other again. Ikenna did not have a moment to collect himself before Tochi grasped at his arms. Ikenna dug his feet into the sand and pulled Tochi forward to counter the weight. Ikenna knew his strategy would last only a moment, but a moment was all he needed. Tochi increased his strength, and Ikenna let go and dropped to his knees. He saw Tochi begin to fall forward, and Ikenna decided to help him on the way down. He grasped Tochi's calves and rolled to the side, bringing the larger man with him. Ikenna heard a heavy thud, and bits of sand and dust got in his mouth. He knew he had won.

He felt hands reaching for him almost immediately, and next thing he knew, he was being carried by a group of men, and the crowd was cheering for him. A drummer had joined the flute player, and they both followed behind as the men carried Ikenna in a circle. Grinning, Ikenna raised his hands to the delight of the crowd. A few people shouted out, "Di mgba!" and Ikenna grinned wider at the title. He was the best wrestler. He had done it.

That night, after the celebration was over, Ikenna lay on his back, wide awake but with his eyes closed. He could still hear the drums. He could see the ring and feel the energy of the crowd. It was like he was still there. He opened his eyes and realized he had reached his hands out in front of him. His elder brother, Odera, stirred awake from his movements.

"What's going on? Are you okay?" Odera was half asleep, but he reached out across their shared sleeping mat to pat his brother on the head. "It's going to be okay, eh, no matter what it is; we'll talk about it tomorrow." He did not wait for an answer—or maybe he could not—before he was right back asleep.

Ikenna chuckled and shook his head. His eldest brother liked to give advice he had not asked for, but Ikenna knew Odera did it because he worried. As the eldest, he felt responsible for everything that happened in Ikenna's life. Ikenna was glad he was the younger one, because the alternative seemed like a hard job. Odera's interruption was enough of a distraction to allow Ikenna to fall asleep. He did not wake up until he felt someone shaking him.

"Huh, what's happening?" He sat up with his heart racing, but it slowed down once his brother's face came into view.

Odera smiled at his brother and said, "Di mgba, our wrestler. You're awake? After you get ready, go and fetch some firewood; there's little left."

Ikenna nodded and stood up to prepare for his day. Odera left after waking him up, and Ikenna knew he would not be back until much later.

Odera spent his day hunting or helping their father with the farm. By the time he returned home, he was too tired to do anything else. When Odera was younger, he used to take Ikenna into the forest and teach him the names of trees or how to spot certain animals. Now Ikenna went to the forest alone.

It was hard to gather firewood, but Ikenna had been doing it for so long that he did not have to think too hard while he worked. He left his compound well into the morning, his ax in one hand, his basket in the other. Across his body, he wore a woven raffia bag. When he arrived at the forest, he started looking for dead trees. Ikenna knew to select already drying trees and cut off dry and dead branches from living trees. Odera had always warned him not to take the trees that were still green. As time passed, Ikenna's arms hurt enough that he needed to take a break. He opened his traveling bag and pulled out a few pieces of boiled yam that had been wrapped in banana leaves. They were cold by now, but hunger is the best seasoning. Once he was done eating, he pulled out a small flute from his bag. Ikenna enjoyed the way music helped him relax. He brought the flute to his lips and blew, mixing between long and short notes. As Ikenna played, the music seemed to blend into the forest, becoming another part of its sound.

Then Ikenna heard a curious sound coming from deeper in the forest. It sounded like drumming. Before he realized it, Ikenna was walking toward the sound and leaving his basket behind. Ikenna did not notice, but the air around him began to warp, and the trees, grass, and other material things became more like mirages. Ikenna heard the drums beating faster with each step he took. Just as he was about to break into a run, he tripped.

Brushing against the ground was enough to shake him out of the trance. He investigated the space ahead of him, and the trees were lined up, almost inviting him to walk farther. Ikenna turned around. Every few trees he stopped to make a small mark—he did not know when but he knew he would be coming back.

When Ikenna found his basket, he quickly gathered up the short, round logs of wood. He would split them when he returned to his family's compound. The walk back passed without Ikenna's full awareness. He was still thinking about the strange events that had happened earlier and the drums he had heard. When he arrived home, there were visitors all through the compound. Big iron pots sat in a circle around individual cooking fires. Ikenna saw several members of his family, including his parents and his brother, around different fires. Some people were making soups, while others fried or boiled yams. Upwind from the fires, but within an arm's length, two men stood next to large mortars and were holding long pestles. Every so often, one of the children by the fire would transfer the boiled yam from the pot to the mortar, and the men pounded it ceaselessly. Eventually, when it reached a smooth, even texture, they would mold it into round, white balls and serve it with some of the soup being cooked. Once, Ikenna tried helping with the pounded yam, but the serving he made was so full of seeds—small bits of cool yam that did not blend in—that he was the only one who could eat it. Now he just stayed to do what he did best—eat.

Ikenna saw two of his cousins splitting wood in the back of one of the compound buildings. Because the food was not ready, he walked over to join them. They waved when they saw him approach.

"Ike, come and help us finish this pile." Though they were in the same age grade, his cousin Dube was taller and leaner than he was. Like his father, he was learning how to tap wine. Every morning, before the rooster crowed, he would go into the forest with his father to climb the tall palm trees barefoot and supported only by cords of twine. As a result, his feet grew calloused and hard, and his body lean and limber. Even though he was strong enough to climb, he still struggled with the logs of wood. Ikenna, who was shorter and stockier in comparison, could chop the wood easier than Dube could.

"So he should do your own and then do his own? You don't have shame?" Ikenna's other cousin Amobi interjected. His build was more like Ikenna's, though he was not as bulky. His father was a trader and would travel between communities to sell the things the people in his compound grew or made. He was the most widely traveled of everyone in their age grade. Whenever he came back, he would regale them with stories of his adventures. When he was not traveling with his father, he would fish to support his family.

"Amobi, why are you disturbing my peace? Who sent you? Tell them you can't find me, oh!"

Before they could continue going back and forth, Ikenna interrupted. "Okay, okay, both of you, stop." Ikenna shook his head and shoved Dube aside, taking his place by the chopping block.

"I'll do it, but bring palm wine for my father next time, eh?"

Dube nodded and placed his hands on Ikenna's shoulders. "Thank you , thank you. There's really nothing better than a brother."

Ikenna laughed and rolled his eyes. Amobi sucked his teeth and kept chopping his own pile. Dube sat against the house wall, between Amobi and Ikenna. Amobi tried to ignore Dube, but the other boy started throwing small pieces of rock at him. They did not hurt, but it was enough to annoy him. Every time another rock hit, Amobi's eye twitched.

"Amobi, sorry now, you know I'm not strong." Dube waved his limbs around as if to demonstrate. "You're not angry, right?"

"How will I know whether I'm angry or not when I can't even think?" Suddenly Amobi grabbed one of the pebbles that had fallen on his chopping block and threw it back at Dube. "You don't know how to be quiet when somebody is upset?" At this point, he could not hide the laugh in his voice. He and Dube were related to Ikenna from different sides of his family, but they had all hung out together since childhood. He was used to Dube's antics by now, but he did not want to laugh and encourage his habits.

Dube shook his head. "No I don't know, sorry. I'll have to bother you." He stood and walked toward Amobi, who started to retreat.

"What are you doing?"

"Nothing, nothing. I already said I don't know how to leave somebody alone, so sorry in advance." Dube's face took on a sharp, almost wicked change that contradicted the laughter in his eyes.

"Dubenna, stay away from me. Ikenna, see your cousi—… ahh!" Amobi gave a startled yelp. While he was talking, Dube had jumped out of nowhere. Amobi turned to avoid the crash, but the Dube ended up on his back. Amobi barely had time to think "this is going to hurt" before he and Dube crashed down into the ground.

"I won! I won!" Dube raised his hands in mock victory and looked to Ikenna for confirmation. "I won, right?"

"If it was that simple, then I might as well never wrestle again." Ikenna kept chopping his wood, undisturbed by the chaos of his cousins.

"Get off me," Amobi grumbled.

"Are you okay?" Dube stood and then reached to help Amobi up.

"You're asking after you tackled me?" Amobi took his hand to stand up and then brushed the sand off his body.

"Sorry, sorry, forgive me. I was trying to make you laugh." Even though Dube said he was sorry, he did not sound like he was. In fact, he sounded like he was laughing. No, he was definitely laughing. Ikenna shook his head in mock exasperation.

"Dubenna, leave Amobi alone before that ax flies at your head." Ikenna did not think Amobi was angry, but sometimes one person's jokes hurt someone else. He did not want to take the chance.

"I'm not angry," Amobi said, as if he had read Ikenna's mind, and Dube grinned in relief. "Well, I'm not angry about you asking Ikenna to chop the wood. I'm angry you tackled me to the ground!" He tapped Dube on the side of his head lightly. "Bring me palm wine next time too."

Dube nodded, his head bobbing like a lizard.

Ikenna and Amobi kept cutting the rest of the wood, and Dube let them. He entertained himself by drawing lines in the sand or occasionally commenting on how much better Ikenna and Amobi did at chopping firewood.

"See, Ikenna you're going even faster than me. It's better I even asked you. If you waited for me, it would take longer. By the time we finished, all the food would be gone."

He nodded after he spoke, as if he had done something grand.

Amobi and Ikenna ignored him.

"Ike, why did it take you so long to come back this time? You usually arrive first." Amobi asked.

Ikenna explained the strange encounter in the forest to his cousins, and they listened in rapt attention. When he was done, they all fell silent. Finally, Dube spoke.

"I've heard a story about spirits wrestling."

Amobi nodded and asked Ikenna, "You said you heard drums? Did they sound like wrestling drums?"

Ikenna's eyes grew wide. Spirit wrestling? He could not imagine the challenge.

"I think so, but I don't know. I don't remember a lot of it. I'll go back tomorrow to look." Ikenna was excited. He had not expected to be the best in his age grade so soon, and he was worried about becoming bored, but wrestling spirits would never be boring.

"Wait, that might be dangerous," Amobi said, frowning. "You don't know what could happen to you."

"Whatever it is, I bet it would be exciting." Ikenna shrugged off Amobi's caution. It was not that he did not think there was danger, but he thought the spirits were calling for him. He felt it. Whatever was there, even danger, was for him to meet.

"Dube, Ikenna, Amobi, the food is ready!" Ikenna's mother called out.

Ikenna and Amobi dropped their axes and dusted off their hands, while Dube got to his feet. They walked to the food pots and grabbed servings of pounded yam and soup.

The rest of the day was spent in lazy merriment. Everyone was too full or tired from the festivities of the previous day, and as daylight faded, so did their energy.

Odera returned home at the last light. He walked into the room he shared with Ikenna and found his younger brother still awake, staring at the ceiling.

"What are you hoping to find up there?"

"Adventure," Ikenna responded without looking away.

Odera grunted and lay down next to Ikenna. "Adventure doesn't put food in your belly or a roof over your head."

"Yes, but it puts breath in my body," Ikenna said with a smile.

Odera swatted him on the stomach. "And lack of rest can take it out of you. Why are you thinking so hard?"

Ikenna shrugged. "I feel like I have a choice to make, but I don't know what to choose."

Odera stayed quiet for a moment before he responded. "I think, out of everything, the thing that gives breath would be most important."

Ikenna did not say anything, and eventually both boys fell asleep.

Ikenna's dreams were foggy and disjointed. He dreamt of drums and wrestling. At some point he thought he heard his brother's voice.

"Ikenna, you can only be who you are, nothing else." Then he felt a warmth on his forehead that he recognized as his brother's hand before it disappeared, and he fell back asleep.

When he woke up, he knew what he was going to do. Without telling anyone, he sneaked out of his compound and headed back to the forest. He walked to the last place he remembered and started searching around until he found his tree markings. After that, it was easy to figure out the direction he had run toward the day before. Ikenna started to retrace his steps. His pace quickened with each step. Soon he was running as fast as he could through the forest, his arms deftly sweeping aside the branches that popped up in front of him.

Then he heard the music. Ikenna picked up his pace, and this time he noticed the air around him start to warp. He did not stop moving. The sound of drums, flutes, and chanting grew louder. Eventually there were no trees left—just a swirl of blues and greens and yellows. Then there was nothing. Ikenna stepped into the darkest night he had ever witnessed. His body seemed to float in a sea of nothingness. He blinked, and then he was tumbling into soft earth. Something lifted him up, but no one was touching him. He stood up and a crowd of spirits filled his gaze. Some had two, or even four, heads. Others had torsos that matched the length of their limbs, as well as wings, tails, and horns. Ikenna knew that he had more than enough reasons to be scared, but all he felt was excitement.

"You've come!" A booming voice rang out and the crowd of spirits parted. Ikenna's attention was drawn to a short, two-faced spirit who had three legs and was walking out from the crowd.

"Were you the one who called me?" Ikenna's voice was clear, tinged only with the surges of excitement he still felt.

The crowd laughed and the two-faced spirit answered, "Only one spirit has the authority to call you here, but you cannot meet them yet. Come with me."

The spirit started walking back into the crowd, and Ikenna followed. Soon he could not see out from the swarm of spirits around him.

"What do I need to do to earn the right?"

As Ikenna asked the question, he walked through the last of the crowd and met a sight more familiar than home, a wrestling circle.

"By fighting, of course." The two-faced spirit walked into the center of the ring. "You need to win three fights; then you can meet the spirit that brought you here."

Learning that he was going to wrestle erased any thoughts of his summoner from Ikenna's head. He walked into the circle without further ado and looked around at the crowd of spirits.

"Who wants to go first?"

The answer was a spirit with six arms. It strode into the ring, supported by a flared-up crowd.

"Otutu." He announced himself with a single word—his name. The match had not started, so Ikenna and Otutu stared at each other. The two-faced spirit stood between them, serving as a barrier to hold back the building tension.

"Okay, once I leave the circle, you can start." The spirit backed out of the court and like lightning, Otutu struck.

It charged toward Ikenna, striking from the left with all three of its arms. Ikenna did the opposite of what the crowd expected and ran toward Otutu. As its arms came toward him in an attempt to pull him down, Ikenna moved to the right and pushed his arms out. Instead of being pulled down or pushed off his feet, he was pulled toward Otutu. Ikenna hoped his arms would act as force to push the spirit down, but Otutu was sturdy. It resisted the push and they ended up in a grapple.

Ikenna dropped to one knee, surprising the spirit. He felt Otutu's arms on his shoulders, attempting to lift him up, but that just gave Ikenna an opportunity. He wrapped his arms behind Otutu's left knee and pulled up as he stood. Otutu had been trying to pick him up, so Ikenna stood easily, and the force was too much for Otutu. The spirit tripped and landed on its back. Ikenna smiled at his victory and stretched out his arms.

"Who's next?"

Otutu huffed and walked out of the circle without looking at Ikenna. The boy smiled. He had not realized spirits could be sore losers.

"Felele, you're next!" The two-faced spirit called up a spirit from the crowd.

His next opponent was a feathered creature. Its face was covered in white chalk, with feathers growing out the side like a winged sun. It had long arms that grew short, soft feathers on the inside and longer, fuller ones on the outside. Its legs were similarly covered and extended into talon feet. Like Otutu, Felele did not talk.

When the two-faced spirit left the ring, this time Ikenna did not hesitate to move. He assumed Felele was going to come at him, and he was right. When the spirit reached its right arm forward to grab at him, Ikenna twisted to the left and grabbed the inside of the arm coming at him. When he managed to stop the arm, he did not stop moving and continued pulling to the left. Felele adjusted and followed the force of Ikenna's pull to keep his balance. It moved its other arm in the same direction its body was being pulled, hoping to lock Ikenna into a grapple. It worked and the two came to a standstill, holding each other in place by the forearm. Felele pushed forward, and Ikenna bent and widened his stance as he backed up. While pushing his arms out, he ducked lower so that his head was parallel to the spirit's chest. The move shifted Felele's balance, and when the spirit tried to rebalance, Ikenna abruptly let go of Felele's arms and tackled the spirit from the torso. The two of them ended up on the floor, with Ikenna pinning the spirit to the ground. He stood and extended an arm to the spirit, who took it and then clapped him on the back, before leaving the circle.

The next challenger did not need to be introduced. It was a short, four-headed spirit with scaly skin and a long tail. It hit its hand on its chest three times.

"I am Okiri! Ikenna, you will fall today."

Ikenna laughed and shrugged his shoulders. He knew this was his last fight before he got to meet the spirit that called him here. He was not going to give up now.

"If you're so certain, why are you talking? The sand is right here," Ikenna responded. Then he walked up to Okiri until they were less than an arm's-length apart. The two wrestlers sunk into deep squats. When the two-faced spirit gave the go-ahead, Ikenna reached out to grab Okiri's arms, but the spirit pushed out at him instead. As he staggered back, Ikenna was able to grab onto Okiri's right wrist. Ikenna regained his balance and wrapped his arm around Okiri's shoulders. He pushed his feet into the ground and lifted Okiri. The spirit came up with him. Ikenna was surprised by its lightness. After successfully lifting both its feet off the ground, he set down Okiri.

Okiri sighed and shook his head at the result. His had ended up being the quickest and easiest match. "Take the next round too," he said as he walked out of the circle. No one took his place.

Ikenna turned to the two-faced spirit and asked, "What happens now? Where is the spirit that called me?"

The two-faced spirit handed Ikenna a single ukwa nut and said, "Eat first. Then you will wrestle."

Ikenna eyed the nut. He was not sure what it could do to sustain him, but he threw it in his mouth. His body was filled with a rush of energy, and the aches from his previous fights started to fade. He did not understand how something so small could be so helpful, but he was grateful.

"Thank you."

Nodding, the two-face spirit said, "It's time."

At the spirits' words, a hush spread through the crowd. Even the drummers and flute players stopped playing. The silence was not flat—it was charged. As moments passed, the air seemed to compress more tightly until Ikenna felt its heaviness as a physical pressure. Then he was drawn to the sound of rattling beads. A spirit walked out from the crowd. It was shirtless, wearing only a short wrapper. It had red coral anklets on each leg, and a wooden mask covered its face. Its skin was decorated in white chalk, with circular patterns across its chest and straight lines down its back and limbs.

Ikenna felt his back cool down, and he shook his head to focus his thoughts. As the spirit walked into the ring, the flute player started to blow a single, long tone. The drummers started a slow, deep rhythm. After the two-faced spirit left, Ikenna and his opponent began circling each other. The spirit darted forward toward Ikenna, but Ikenna easily bent his body back, avoiding the grapple. Likewise, when Ikenna reached out to grab the spirit by the sides, it evaded him by stepping back. Ikenna opened his grip and pushed the spirit back instead, making it teeter. The spirit adjusted and grabbed Ikenna's wrists before he could pull away. Ikenna felt himself tumbling forward, and so he dug his feet into the sand and pulled back. The spirit followed Ikenna's pull and fell to one knee. It let go of Ikenna's wrists as it fell, wrapping both arms around Ikenna's right leg. The spirit tried to use the force of his shoulder to throw Ikenna, who leaned forward and pushed into the spirit instead of falling backward. The spirit grunted and pushed up, keeping Ikenna across its shoulders. It stood completely, taking Ikenna with him. Ikenna's mind blanked. The spirit rotated, basking in the cheers of the crowd before he set Ikenna down.

"You've lost. I don't have anything else to say to you. Leave."

Regaining clarity, Ikenna swallowed to get rid of the hard, sharp stone that seemed to have lodged itself in his throat. He could not believe he had lost. Well, of course he lost. He had come to fight with spirits. Who did he think he was? Maybe they had even been playing with him this entire time. Maybe he had not won any of the matches, really.

Wait. He stopped to examine his thoughts. Did one loss erase everything he had done? No, the loss was its own lesson. It had never happened before, and Ikenna had experienced something new. Was he not still alive? Could he not keep going? In fact, the only person who could stop him was himself. As his thoughts crystallized, everything became clear. Ikenna realized that it would be okay if he wanted to stop. He could rest, he could stop wrestling. He just did not want to.

Ikenna grinned and stepped back into the circle. "Again."

A change happened in the spirit. It gave off waves of brilliant blue energy. Ikenna looked down and realized that he was giving off a bright-red light. Not only that, but he also felt stronger and faster than he had ever been before. His mind was clear, and he could feel each move before it happened. He stopped thinking. When the spirit tried to pull him down to the ground, Ikenna would throw his body into the movement, dragging the spirit down as well until it let go or adjusted.

When the spirit adjusted, Ikenna would fall toward the spirit, using as much energy as he could manage to try to push it down. It did not work. The spirit backed away too quickly for Ikenna to destabilize it. As they wrestled, their movements looked like dancing. By this time, the energy of both wrestlers merged and flowed through both of them. Their wrestling circle was bathed in their glow. Ikenna widened his squat stance and held his arms out in front of him. The spirit did the same.

They circled each other some more in silence before Ikenna grabbed one of the spirit's arms. When the spirit tried to jerk back, Ikenna allowed himself to be pulled in and rammed his side into the spirit's chest. Stepping back from the impact, the spirit lost its balance, but did not fall. Ikenna lunged forward again, but the spirit had expected that. It moved to the side as it stepped back, and when Ikenna came toward it, the spirit used his momentum to stabilize itself. They ended up in a close grapple with their knees bent. Ikenna pushed up and tightened his grip, feigning an attempt to stand. Predictably, the spirit countered the force. Ikenna jerked down and, using the force of the spirit's momentum, he twisted to the side and flipped the spirit on its back. He had won.

Ikenna helped the spirit stand, and they faced each other. The spirit pulled off his mask, and Ikenna found himself staring at his own face. He realized this spirit was his chi. The spirit did not wait to confirm it.

"I am Chi-Ike. You deserve to know my name."

The spirit stared into Ikenna's eyes in silence. Then Ikenna heard its voice in his head.

"Strength is not acceptance of an impossible burden. Strength is not the thing that bubbles over in times of victory. Strength is not pain; it is not pushing past what you can do—that is self-deception. Strength is the will to carry on. Strength is life, the burning fire that wakes you up in the morning and urges you to live, simply because you want to. Where you find that fire is where you find your strength. For your strength, you have been permitted to enter the spirit world with your flesh body. With our strength, we will hold our people. As long as we keep going so can our people."

Chi-Ike flashed a grin that matched Ikenna's and said out loud, "Again."

Ikenna wrestled in the spirit world to his heart's content. He grew stronger every time and so did his chi. The two of them remain locked in an unending cycle.

Messenger birds and spirits that could go between the realms spread the story of Ikenna's circumstance. People were impressed by his feats, so Igbo people started using wooden figures, ikenga, to hold the spirit of their willpower.

They would buy the carved dolls at a market and ask a dibìà to consecrate them, calling down the willpower they needed to achieve their destiny. Soon the practice spread throughout Igboland.

CHAPTER 6
OJIUGO—
THE RARE GEM

It was nighttime, and the community of Izu was quiet. In the dark, Urenna held a small torch in his left hand as he walked next to his younger brother, Somadina, who was carrying a small bow across his back. Somadina's age grade had their 10th ceremony the month before, so he was ready to keep watch for the first time, and Urenna's job was to keep him safe, just in case. The night watch was present because even Chineke used one eye for daylight and another eye for night, so people should keep an eye open at night too—or at least that was what their father said. Urenna was six years older and had long passed the age of keeping watch; his age group was in charge of hunting instead. As they walked, they saw some of Somadina's friends, but they did not stop to talk. It would be dangerous to draw attention to themselves. Urenna and Somadina spoke sporadically in low voices.

"I thought something was going to happen," Somadina murmured, glancing around him. Besides his brother and the other watchers, they were alone.

"That's a good thing. If you ask for trouble, trouble will come to you," Urenna said, without looking at his brother. "It's better to have peace."

Somadina nodded, but he still peered into the night intently, ready to respond to anything that cared to come toward Izu. Urenna smiled and continued walking in silence. His brother's behavior was necessary too.

"Ure, are you getting married?"

Urenna jerked and glanced down at his brother. "Why are you asking that?"

"My mother said you were getting married soon, and I should look at what you were doing, because it would be my turn soon."

Urenna shook his head. "Don't think about that. I'm not doing anything."

"You're not getting married?"

"No I am." Urenna pulled out a small kola nut the color of ivory from his traveling bag. "But I'm waiting for this. Ojiugo. Then I will get married."

"You're going to marry a kola nut?"

Urenna laughed and put the kola nut back in his bag before he ruffled his brother's hair. "Exactly. A very precious one."

The brothers finished their walk in silence, ending it just as the first signs of light began to show. They made their way back to their compound, one of the largest in Izu. Their father was a titled man, and each of his two wives carried titles as well, so their compound was big enough for five or six families. It was surrounded by a red soil wall decorated with ùlì. The brothers entered through the wooden gates that had been left ajar. They washed themselves with water from the pots outside before they went into their room and collapsed, exhausted, onto their sleeping mats.

Urenna woke up not long after, sleep still trying to force his eyes closed. Somadina was snoring on a mat next to him, his limbs stretched out. Urenna considered waking him up, but he decided to give him more time to sleep. Instead, he followed his morning ritual, consulting with his chi and then his ancestors before stepping out of his room. It did not take long for someone to be aware of his presence.

"Urenna, you're up? Your father is looking for you." His father's younger brother, Eke, jogged up to him. "Did you sleep well? You seem tired."

"Eeh, thank you, Uncle. I'll go now." Urenna yawned. "I was with Som last night, so I'm still tired."

Eke tsked in pity. "Okay, rest early today, enh?" He jogged off, and Urenna went to meet his father.

He made his way to his father's òbu. When he entered, he was greeted by three people: his father, his mother, and Zara, Somadina's mother and his father's second wife.

His father, Okoye, smiled when he saw Urenna walk in. "Okpara, you've arrived. I want to talk to you. Come and sit down."

Urenna sat, and they broke kola. Then Okoye explained. "In three days, Ora is going to be celebrating the might of their wrestlers. They are asking everyone surrounding them to send wrestlers. I want you to go."

Ora was one of the communities next to Izu. The two communities had lived next to each other and traded for longer than anyone could remember. It was common to host competitions or displays between them. Dancers and wrestlers from Ora would come to Izu festivals too.

Urenna nodded. "Of course."

His mother, Golibe, chimed in. "We want you to take your brother too. He will learn from the journey. Let him grow well." Urenna looked at Somadina's mother, Zara, who nodded in agreement.

"Yes, a well-traveled child is wiser than the oldest person. He shouldn't just stay at home. Remember, I have a brother in Ora. You can stay with him when you go."

Okoye added, "You heard them, Urenna. Take your brother and go. Make sure to look after him."

Urenna agreed, and he was about to ask for permission to leave when his mother spoke.

"Nna, will you not take a wife?" Urenna looked at his father, but Okoye pretended not to see him.

"Well, when I find a wife, I will bring her back," Urenna said, finally.

"You don't need to find one!" Golibe exclaimed. "How many people have sent us requests about a marriage? You can choose a wife right now. If it continues like this, would we not be insulting them?"

Zara stepped in to speak for Urenna. "Nné, to marry is not a simple thing. He can't just choose a wife like that." She paused. "But Ure, you really should start looking. Have you not found anyone?"

Urenna shook his head. "Mma, my father was lucky. He just had to leave his house and he found not just one but two eagles. But he forgot to leave the blessing for me, so I haven't been as lucky. Maybe if you send a message to your kind, they will look out for me?" He said the last bit with a smile, and his mother sucked in her teeth in mock annoyance, while Zara laughed.

"If you have that mouth, you won't have a problem finding a wife. Don't make your mother worry too much, eh?"

Urenna nodded and said his good-byes. He was glad to have escaped the questioning intact.

Two days later, Urenna and Somadina joined a group of wrestlers heading to Ora. The journey would take the whole day so they were setting out early. Along with their personal items, most people brought animals to help them carry the heavier things. Somadina led their donkey, while Urenna joined the older men to guard the traveling group. They took short breaks for water and rest, but they managed to make it through the bush-path to get to Ora before dark.

They were welcomed warmly, and the group split up to find the people they knew.

Zara's brother, Ossai, met them at the town's entrance. He smiled at them in delight when he spotted them.

"Ah, is it Urenna and Somadina? The last time I saw you, Ure, you were not even to my chest, now you've come to wrestle, enh? Somadina, you were still crying to stay with your mother. Now look at you, smiling. You've grown. Come, let me take you inside."

They greeted Ossai and followed him to his compound. They would stay in the same rooms as his sons—Urenna with the older ones, Somadina with the younger ones. Ossai's wife, Simdi, had prepared a meal for them, and so they ate with the family before going to sleep.

The festival began the next morning. Urenna and his brother joined Ossai's family and the rest of Ora as they swarmed to the center of the community.

They found a place to sit and waited for the event to start. Once everyone was settled, the eldest titled person in Ora, a man named Afam, started the festivities.

The first group of people to perform were the musicians. They played their drums and flutes so quickly that Urenna was almost dizzy watching them. Somadina clapped his hands in excitement at each music group. Then came the story-tellers. Each person tried to engage the audience, and some were more successful than others. The most popular story was about a father and son who tried to journey from one place to another with their donkey. On the way, they would be stopped by passers-by who would comment on how they chose to travel. Some would say the son was disrespectful for letting the father walk; others would say the father was careless when his son let him ride their donkey and the son walked instead. Eventually, the pair realized that if they never stopped listening to everyone's opinion, they would never finish their journey. The crowd clapped in approval of a good story. The least favorite story was about a fishing competition, but the storyteller did not engage the crowd, and so they sent him off before he finished. He took the crowd's rejection good-naturedly and promised to be back with a better story.

Then it was Urenna's turn. Somadina was not wrestling, so Urenna left him with Ossai and went to stand with the wrestlers. He was given a shorter wrapper to wear, and his bare chest was decorated with nzu before the fights started. He was not the first to fight, so he waited with the others. Urenna knew he was not the best wrestler, but he saw himself as one of the best. The people he saw fighting made him doubt that. Either way, Urenna would find out whether he was good soon. When it was his turn, he won his first match easily. His opponent was bigger than he was but slower, so Urenna tripped him. His next opponent was a harder challenge, and he faced the opposite problem—it was he who was bigger and slower. He almost lost. Then he decided to anticipate where his opponent would go next instead of chasing him. His decision won him his match. His next match was not as fortunate. Urenna put up a good fight, but his opponent was more skilled. They were locked in a grapple for a long time before Urenna's strength gave out and his opponent flipped him. Urenna laughed and shook his head. He was not too upset because he knew he did his best, but he was going to train more.

When he returned to his seat, his brother was staring at him with wide eyes, and his uncle clapped him on his back.

"Good work, you did not disgrace your father."

"Ure, can you teach me more when we go back home? I'm going to surprise everyone when I wrestle again. I'll be as strong as you!"

Urenna thanked his uncle and then shook his head at his brother. "Som, I've already cleared my own path; yours is still waiting for you. You can check to see where I stumbled and avoid it. You have to be better than me, enh?"

"Okay!"

They settled in to watch the rest of the fights. Urenna found out the name of the person he lost to—Dike—who ended up winning the competition after two more fights. Urenna cheered with the others.

After the wrestlers came the dancers. First, the warriors of Ora performed their dance. The ground beneath them trembled and spat up dust as they moved. Urenna shivered in fright and awe as he watched them. He was a hunter, but he had never been in battle. War was something else. Unlike Izu, Ora was right by the coast, so they had to defend their community from people sneaking in through the rivers that cut through their town. Ora's strong defense also protected many of the inland communities like Izu, which was part of why they had such a strong bond. Ora had mostly fishermen because it did not have a lot of land; therefore, Izu provided much of Ora's produce.

After the warriors, different dance groups came up to perform. One of them caught Urenna's eye—specifically, one of the dancers did. She did not stand out. She was not taller or shorter than the other dancers, so Urenna was not sure why he had noticed her. But once he did, he could not look away. He leaned over to his uncle and asked, "Who is that?"

"You mean Amara?" His uncle was quick to respond with a smile. When Urenna nodded, he continued, "That is Ézè Onochie's daughter. She's one of the most talented dancers in Ora, and people say she will take a yam title, like her mother too." Ossai eyed Urenna. "Come to think of it, aren't you looking for a wife? What? Are you interested? You want me to introduce you?"

Urenna shook his head hard. "No, no. Please don't. I was just wondering."

Ossai did not seem convinced, but he allowed Urenna to stop talking about it.

After the dancers came Somadina's favorite part: the people of Ora filled the performance space with pots of food and water. After the elders took some food, Somadina rushed Urenna and Ossai to the center, and they grabbed bowls of food. As they were getting their food, Urenna saw Amara walk up next to them.

He cleared his throat and said, "I saw your dancing." When she looked up and smiled, he continued, "It was really good."

"Thank you." Her voice was as thick as fire smoke but as light as clouds.

Urenna was about to walk away when Amara said, "I like your wrestling." She laughed. "It's not as good as my dancing, but it's not bad."

Urenna scratched his head. If he had known he would meet her, he would have fought harder. He was so lost in thought, he almost missed the rest of her words.

"You must be really good at the thing you actually do."

"What?"

"I mean, you're clearly not a wrestler, yet you did really well. You have enough talent to be a wrestler if you choose, but you chose something else?" Her voice held amusement and Urenna realized he was being complimented.

"Oh, yes. I … I hunt. A group of us do, but I lead the group. He could not keep the pride out of his voice as he finished. He kept his people fed. From the look on Amara's face, she agreed he should be proud.

Their conversation was interrupted by someone behind them trying to get food. "The talk is sweet, but it will not expire if you wait. Our food will get cold. Nnà, let us eat, enh?"

Urenna laughed in embarrassment and moved aside to let the people behind him eat. Amara smiled at him and left to join her friends. His uncle and brother had since returned to their seats, so he joined them.

"You were just wondering?" Ossai asked when Urenna got within hearing range.

"I liked her dancing," Urenna responded, but his uncle just smiled.

"I've heard that one before."

They ate and then returned to Ossai's compound after the feast. Urenna and Somadina returned to Izu the next day.

Back in Izu, time passed, but Urenna could not stop thinking about Amara. He did not know anything about her, but he wanted to, and so he volunteered to take the next set of goods to Ora. Usually Eke would do it, but Urenna did not want to give up the chance to see Amara. Okoye agreed, so Urenna made the trip the day before Ora's big market day, along with his donkey and baskets of produce. He stayed with Ossai like before, but this time, Ossai's wife led him to the market the next day. Simdi showed Urenna where to set up his wares and left him to tend to her own trade. Ossai was a fisherman, so she sold some of his catch, as well as the small amount of produce she could grow. While people gathered around him, Urenna kept an eye out for Amara. Eventually he saw her. She was with an older woman—her mother, Urenna guessed—so he had not seen her at first. She was handing out goods and talking to customers, while her mother handled the items people gave them in exchange. Unlike the other sellers from Ora, whose goods were mostly fish, Amara and her mother were selling different yams, beans, and even rice. They had more produce than some of the traders from Izu. Urenna whistled in appreciation. They were clearly skilled farmers. They had come in much later than the other traders, but by the end of the market day they had sold everything they brought. Urenna had sold everything as well, so he stacked his empty baskets together and secured them on the donkey.

"I haven't seen you in our market before."

Urenna turned his head at the familiar voice, almost tripping in the process. "Amara!"

She raised her eyebrows. "You know my name?"

"Ah, yes … my uncle told me last time."

She laughed. "I know, I'm joking. Urenna, the hunter."

"You know my name?"

"Yes, your uncle told me."

Urenna laughed. "Next time I'll bring him five chickens."

"Next time?"

Urenna nodded. "I'll be bringing the goods instead of my uncle. It would be good to learn to do this for when I have my own children to raise."

Amara hummed but did not comment. She then said, "My mother left with the other women for a meeting. It's not dark, but I don't want to walk back alone. Come with me?"

"Of course." Urenna gestured to his donkey. "Do you want to go back on the donkey? It would be easier than walking."

Amara shook her head. "No, you would have to carry everything. But can I add my baskets? They are empty too."

Urenna agreed immediately, and they headed back empty-handed, while the donkey carried their baskets. They walked in relative silence, sharing only a few things about their families and their parents, and how many siblings they had. Amara had four brothers and a younger sister. Urenna hated that he could not think of anything important to say. He walked her to the gates of her compound and then turned around and headed to Ossai's home.

Weeks and then months passed like this. Urenna would travel to Ora for trade, and somehow Amara would need an escort back. As they got to know each other, their relationship grew into a friendship and maybe, Urenna thought, something else. He decided to find out.

"Amara." This day was like any other big market day, except it was not. Today, Urenna had something important to say.

"Urenna," she responded.

He smiled. He was used to the way she talked by now, but he still found it funny. "Amara, you know, my mother wants me to take a wife." He hesitated when he sensed Amara stiffen beside him. Maybe he understood their relationship entirely wrong.

"You're taking a wife?" Her voice was flat in a way he had not heard before.

"No. I mean, yes? If you want?" This was not what he had rehearsed.

Amara seemed to realize something, and then her mouth twitched as if she were forcing back a smile. "Urenna, what are you trying to tell me?"

Urenna took a breath. This was his moment. "I have been looking for a wife. Not just because my mother wants me to, but I haven't found anyone that felt right. My parents were happy, and I want to be happy too. And successful," he added, after a beat. "Amara, you're the only person I've met that I can do that with. If you marry me, I swear, Amara, if I bring you any harm, let rain never stop beating my back. Let the ground swallow me. Let Amadịọha…"

"Okay, okay," Amara interrupted him, laughing. "I've heard you. The whole of Ora doesn't have to." She looked at him, mirth still in her eyes. "If I marry you, Ure? I've been talking to you for how long? Do I look like I waste my time?"

Urenna's eyes widened. "So if I talked to your parents…"

"If you didn't, I would be upset." She looked away from him and said, "So stop asking for the ground to take you, because it might as well take me too."

Urenna laughed and did not stop smiling, even when he fell asleep that night.

When Urenna told his parents, his mother cried and danced around the compound. Zara smiled at him, and his father congratulated him and started to gather enough people to visit Amara's parents. They had already known about her—Ossai told them—but it was different coming from Urenna's mouth.

Okoye and Eke went with Urenna to Ora. They brought a small basket of kola and palm wine but not much else. This time, Urenna went into Amara's compound, with his family behind him. Ézè Onochie welcomed them in his òbu, with his wife, Lolo Ndidi. After they broke kola, Okoye explained why they had come.

"Our son has informed us that he wants to bring your daughter to our house," he began. "We came to see if she wanted to come." Okoye was calm. Urenna, however, was wringing his hands together.

Ézè Onochie and Lolo Ndidi looked at each other, and then Ézè Onochie spoke: "We should ask her first then. Amara!"

Urenna assumed she had already been told of their presence because she came into the òbu almost immediately, going to stand next to her parents.

Onochie gestured at Urenna. "Do you know him?"

Amara looked at Urenna. Beads of sweat were collecting on his forehead. She laughed. "Yes, I do."

"Mm..." was all her father said. Urenna swallowed.

Ndidi chimed in. "He says he wants to marry you. How about you?"

Amara smiled. "I feel the same way."

"This child, see how you're smiling." Her mother swatted her gently before shooing her off. "Don't make him nervous. We'll talk after."

When Amara left, Onochie spoke. "We've heard her. Now I want to hear you. Why do you want to marry my daughter?"

Urenna felt the tension leave his body. This was a question he could answer. "I don't know if there's a word for it. I don't know if I can explain it fully, but Amara is the person I've been looking for, and for a long time. She's such an amazing farmer, but she's in a fishing community. In Izu, she can expand her business. I want my business to be making her happy, because her existence makes me happy."

"Ah, the talk is sweet, oh," Ndidi said with a laugh. And for the first time, Onochie broke into a smile.

"My daughter is precious to me. She must be precious to you too."

"She is," Urenna agreed.

"Our son is precious to us," Okoye said, suddenly.

Onochie looked taken aback, and then he smiled and nodded. "Yes, after all, a child is life."

"Don't mind him," Ndidi said. "He knows, that's why he's nervous. Your son is the only thing our daughter sees in her eye, so he's trying to see clearly for her."

Onochie nodded. "That's right, but it's clear to me now that they are both looking at each other. I would be proud to join our families."

Time after that became unrecognizable. Every day was so full and quick, Urenna wondered if it was still the same time he had experienced. If not for the tiredness that dragged his eyes closed at night, Urenna would have thought he had opened them just moments earlier. Before he knew it, Urenna's father gathered the cows, baskets of yams, cloth, and cowry shells to give to Amara's family. Then Urenna met her extended family, and she met his family. Sooner than he expected, his family welcomed Amara and gave her a piece of one of their farmlands, and she moved into Golibe's room. After their wedding, Urenna and Amara would share a side of the compound. The next thing to do would be the wine carrying ceremony, where they would acknowledge each other in front of Amara's family, and receive her father's blessing.

The day before the wine carrying, Amara and Urenna returned to Ora. Urenna and his family stayed with Ossai, and Amara returned to Onochie's compound. The next morning, Urenna and his family, dressed in their finest wrappers and jewelry, walked to Onochie's compound. They were accompanied by musicians announcing their arrival. Onochie greeted and seated them. When the rest of the guests arrived, Onochie broke the kola and greeted everyone. Then Amara came out for the first time. She was wearing two wrappers, one around her chest and the other around her waist. She had a string of red coral around her neck and many beads around her waist. Her skin was decorated in ùlì designs, and her hair was tied in a head wrap. Urenna thought she looked beautiful. Amara greeted the guests and shot a quick smile at Urenna before heading back in. After eating, Urenna hid in the crowd before Amara came out again.

When she stepped out again, Onochie called her to him. He was holding a small gourd of wine.

"There is a man that says he is your husband here."

The crowd laughed, and Amara nodded. Onochie handed her the gourd of palm wine.

"Go and find him."

Amara took the wine and scanned the crowd. Urenna had chosen to sit between two of his cousins. He hoped their similar features would throw her off. For a second, he thought it worked. Amara looked past him as she searched the faces around her, palm wine in hand. Then she whipped around and stared right at him, and he knew she had known where he was from the start. The crowd cheered and the musicians played louder once they realized Amara had found Urenna. She walked to him and squatted so they were eye to eye; then she passed him the gourd filled with palm wine. Urenna took it from her and drank before passing it back. He looked at Amara, and she grinned, showing her teeth. This was his wife. They were married. Urenna smiled back.

CHAPTER 7
WHY THE ALLIGATOR LIVES ALONE

Ngweleaghuli o lacha nbembe kai na!
Olacha!
Ndi gu na fa yi alacha nbembe a na ba si go!
Olacha!

Translation: Alligator, eater of berries, let's leave. The people that came with you to eat berries have left.

In a time of famine in the animal kingdom, seven animals met with a plan. The vulture, who initiated the plan, as well as the crocodile, the pig, the antelope, the dog, the chicken, and the rabbit met in the middle of a forest. All the animals had skin that stretched too thin across their bodies. The vulture and the chicken had patches of skin showing where feathers should have been, and the feathers that did remain were dull and dry. The alligator—the only one of them that could hunt in the rivers—had managed to survive without starving, but he knew he would run out of food soon. More animals had been relying on the waters for nourishment.

The vulture had approached each of them with her plan. As a messenger of Ani, she had the ability to travel through the worlds of the spirit. However, when she was not sending a message from Ani, she did not receive protection for the journey.

The last time the vulture had flown through the spirit world, she had passed a spirit eating mysterious berries; each of them was the size of a chicken egg. The spirit recognized Ani's blessing on her, so they answered her questions. The berry came from a magical tree, the spirit said to the vulture. It had the ability to prevent hunger, and just one berry would allow any animal to survive the famine. The spirit told the vulture where to find the tree, but it was in a direction different from where her message would take her. The vulture wanted to return to find the tree, but she knew she would not have the goddess's blessing the next time she traveled.

Instead, she chose to tell other animals about the tree. They did not have the ability to navigate the spirit world without getting lost, but she could guide them. In exchange, she asked for the protection of the other animals. They agreed without hesitation, but none of them had seen the berries the vulture kept talking about, so a few of them thought it might not be as strong as the vulture claimed. They still wanted to go because any food was worth it.

"Are you sure this will work?" The rabbit hopped in one place to channel his fear.

"There's no reason it shouldn't." The vulture sounded certain. "Just make sure to follow me, and no matter what you do, don't eat anything while we're there."

The berries were spirit food. If the animals ate it while they were in the spirit world, the vulture was not sure they would survive. It would be safer to eat the berries when they returned to the land of beings.

"Does anyone have any questions?" the vulture asked. "If not, stay close to me. Let's go."

The animals did not have any questions, so they huddled next to the vulture and followed her deeper into the forest. It did not take long for darkness to overtake their vision. Even the animals that could see well in the dark found that they could not see farther than the vulture ahead of them. The darkness was not from their world.

"Oh, this is scary." The chicken flapped his wings and glided onto the antelope's back. He would rather watch his surroundings from here than walk.

"You could ask first," the antelope grumbled. He did not press it too hard because having the chicken close was comforting. The spirit world was not a place they should be.

The animals kept walking in silence, and the atmosphere grew scarier with each step. Eventually the vulture broke the silence.

"I think I see it!" She speeded up, and the other animals followed after her.

They arrived together at a slender, tall tree. Its berries were exactly seven in number, and the alligator wondered if it had grown the berries for them. The animals picked one each, and the pig bent to eat his.

"Stop!" The vulture sounded frantic. She swooped toward the pig and covered the berry with her claw. "You don't know what that could do to you."

The pig grew cold. He had forgotten the vulture's warnings. "Thank you, I can't believe I forgot."

The vulture looked at the other animals and reminded them again. "These berries belong to this world. If you eat them here, they might make you of this world too. Be careful."

The animals gathered together and started the journey back to their world. As they walked, the berries started to let off a sweet scent that clouded their senses. The hungry animals felt their stomachs growl, and they groaned. It was bad enough that they had to walk all the way back without eating, but the sweet scent of the berries made resisting even harder.

The alligator walked behind the other animals. As they moved, his mind started to race. He knew the vulture said not to eat the berries, but did she know that it was definitely going to be bad? The more he thought about it, the less likely it seemed. After all, why would the berries be poisonous? The tree had even grown seven ripe berries for them. The alligator made up his mind and ate his berry before the other animals could notice. The moment he swallowed the berry, he felt warmth spread through his body. His stomach was full without being painful and he felt like he had grown stronger. He looked up at the other animals but nothing had changed. He was confident he was right, and the vulture had worried too much.

"Ha, we don't have to endure this torture. The berries are not harmful. I just ate one and I'm fine." The alligator could not keep the brag out of his voice, but the other animals did not even turn around.

"Did you hear me? We don't have to save the berries. We can eat them now." The alligator repeated himself, but it was half-hearted. He could tell something was wrong. He walked up to the other animals, and he moved through them as if he were mist.

"Oh no." The alligator understood that they could not see him. He ran toward the vulture and called out to her, "Can you see me? Can you hear me?" He did not get a response.

The dog was the first one to notice. "Where is the alligator?"

The vulture dived down and turned to face the dog. "What do you mean?"

"The alligator is missing. I don't see him." The dog repeated himself, but he did not need to. The other animals noticed the alligator's absence and panicked. They took turns calling his name, but no one responded.

The alligator saw the animals stopped, and he knew they had noticed his absence. He saw them begin to move around and call out, but he could not hear anything. The alligator's heart sank when he saw the animals begin to walk again. Not knowing what else to do, he followed them.

"Maybe he's already gone back," the dog said, but the pig snorted in response.

"We would have seen him go past us. I think he ate the berry. That's the only explanation. He's gone."

"You don't know that." The chicken did not want the alligator to be hurt, but he had to admit that there did not seem to be any sign of him.

The animals followed the path back through the spirit world, but there was no alligator waiting for them on the other side.

The alligator remained in the spirit world. He had tried to follow the others but an invisible barrier stopped him. He felt like if he kept going he would disappear.

The animals that went to the spirit world survived the famine. The berries sustained them even beyond the famine, but none of them were entirely happy. They felt like the alligator paid a price for them.

In the spirit world, the alligator felt the last of the energy from the berry he had eaten leave him and, with it, his connection to the spirit world. The happy animal ran back through the passage. He had stayed in the spirit world long enough to remember the way out. To his delight, the barrier had disappeared, and he could freely walk back to his world.

The first thing he did was rush to find the other animals. He noticed the fruits on the trees and realized that the famine had passed. The first animal he came across was the antelope. The other animal noticed him, but before the alligator could say anything, he ran away. This continued with every animal the alligator met, and eventually he realized it would never stop. His time in the spirit world had changed him, and the other animals now feared him.

From that day, the alligator and his descendants would live and hunt alone.

CHAPTER 8
THE TORTOISE AND
THE BILLY GOAT

During the rainy season, food is plentiful. The animals are free to eat and drink as they wish, with enough left over for the wise ones to save food for later. In the dry season, food grows scarce. The grass turns brown and the rivers dry up. Animals are left to eat from their stored food or settle with what they can have. At this time, a full belly is rare, but most animals are able to survive until the rains come again.

The goat, Eme, stared at his pile of dried grass. It was all he had managed to save from the season before, but he was not looking forward to surviving on it.

"You don't have to eat it if you don't want to." Mbeku, the tortoise, walked to the pile of grass and poked it with his feet. "In fact, I'm begging you not to eat it." He laughed.

"I don't have much of a choice. No, why are you here? *How* did you get here?" Eme looked behind him and saw that the pile of stones that sectioned off his space had been moved.

"Or, more importantly, how about you eat something that isn't dried grass?" Mbeku countered.

Eme was surprised. He knew the tortoise did not work to gather food all through the rainy season. In fact, the goat had shared his food with Mbeku many times.

"Did you manage to save something? How come I didn't notice?"

"Save?" Mbeku spat the word out as if it were the worst thing he had ever had on his tongue. "Why would I do that? No. I have something better. I have a plan."

With his hooves, Eme nudged Mbeku away from his stored grass. "I'm glad you have a plan, Mbeku, but I'm fine with what I have."

"I'm serious!" Mbeku dropped his voice. "We can go into the spirit world. I found a way."

Eme started. "You found a way into the spirit world?"

Mbeku relaxed, realizing he had Eme's attention. "Yes, and to thank you for helping me, you can come with me!"

"I don't know." Eme was tempted, but the spirit world could be dangerous. He did not know if it was worth the risk.

"Eme, there's nothing to lose. If we don't find anything, we'll go back, but the spirit world reflects this one. They have rain, so there will be food."

Eme knew that Mbeku was right, and he found himself wavering. "Okay, but we won't stay long. If we see any danger, we'll run immediately."

Mbeku laughed. "Definitely, but you'll have to carry me." He gestured with his feet. "I can't go very fast."

"I can do that," Eme agreed. "When do you want to leave?"

"We can go tomorrow. There's no need to wait."

The two animals agreed on a plan, and the next day, they met at the edge of a spirit forest to set out on their journey. The tortoise carried a basket tied to his back, and the goat walked beside him. The tortoise instructed the goat to keep close to him, and they began the long journey to the spirit world. Every so often, Mbeku would look closely at a tree, or a patch of grass, and then nod to himself and keep going.

"What are you doing?" Eme asked.

"Figuring out the path."

Eme wondered if he should question Mbeku's nonanswer, but he was distracted when the grass in front of him began to change colors. The greens and browns of the forest turned into iridescent hues of purples and reds. Soon the air around them shifted to match. They had arrived in the spirit world.

"We did it!" Eme cheered.

"Of course, who do you think I am?" Mbeku was proud of his accomplishment. He did not share that he had followed several vultures through the rainy season. Despite all his hard work, he had been able to figure out only one route, but that one was enough. "Now we just have to find food."

Eme hummed in agreement, and the two friends continued their journey through the spirit forest.

"Wait." Mbeku stopped moving and gestured for Eme to do the same. "What's that in the distance? Smoke?"

Eme looked in the direction of Mbeku's gaze and saw plumes of smoke rising. "I think it is. I'm glad you saw it. Let's go this way." He started walking in a different direction but stopped when he realized Mbeku was not following him.

"What are you doing?" Mbeku asked.

"There's fire. Which means, there's something making fire. We need to leave."

"Or we could head toward it."

"Why would we do that? Mbeku? Mbeku!" Eme quickened his steps and hurried after Mbeku, who had continued to walk toward the smoke.

"They might have food," Mbeku said when Eme caught up to him.

"They could be dangerous," Eme said, remembering to keep his voice low.

"Don't worry, we'll hide first." Mbeku and Eme kept themselves hidden in trees and foliage as they walked toward the cloud of smoke. Eventually they came across a campfire. They ducked behind a cluster of tall, thick trees with full leaves. The camp was simple. There was some sort of meat that Mbeku did not recognize roasting over a low fire. Small mounds of vegetables lay to the side. There were two soft piles of layered grass for sleeping and low-cut logs of wood for seating.

Eme flicked his ears and then dropped to the floor. Mbeku shrunk himself as well as he could. He did not know what the goat had heard, but he wanted to be safe.

"Voices," Eme explained.

As he said that, Mbeku heard them.

"Brother, I'm so hungry. Let's move faster. The sound of heavy footsteps grew louder, and soon a spirit came into view. It walked in from across the area where Mbeku and Eme had hidden, so they could see it clearly. Its face was illuminated by the cooking fire.

The spirit, or rather the spirits, were actually two brothers conjoined at their side. They shared a third leg, and each of their sides sprouted three arms. One brother's head grew out of their neck, while the other grew out of their left shoulder. Their faces were covered with blank, smooth skin except for where it split to mark their mouth. They had no lips, and an eye sat on top of each head. Each set of arms carried a carcass ready to be prepared and cooked.

Mbeku shivered, and he heard Eme swallow beside him. They prayed the spirits would leave quickly.

Something must have been looking out for them, because the brothers made short work of preparing the meat before they set out again.

The brothers walked back in the direction they had come from, and Mbeku saw his chance. Once the brothers were out of sight and their voices disappeared, the tortoise stepped out of his hiding spot and walked toward their campfire.

"Be careful!" Eme called out, his voice a hoarse whisper.

"It's okay. They've left, right?" Mbeku went toward the fire and pulled down the still stick of meat. Without waiting for it to cool off, he took big bites.

Watching his friend eat wore down the rest of Eme's resistance. He headed toward the pile of vegetables and helped himself. The two of them were so invested in eating that they almost missed the sound of the brothers returning.

"Oh no!" Mbeku squirmed out of the basket he was carrying and climbed onto Eme's back as fast as he could make it. The goat took off without looking back, and they had just gotten out of sight when the brothers returned to their camp.

They did not notice it at first, but when they knelt to take a serving of their roasted meat, they realized it was missing.

"Aku, someone stole our food!" the head on the shoulder cried in dismay. They hurried over to their vegetable pile and realized it was mostly gone.

"Who dares? Àkà, don't worry. We will find them." Aku spoke in a grim voice. "They took our food, but they didn't check to make sure they were not eating poison. I put a bell in that meat. If I sing to it, it will call to me. As long as the thief is in this forest, we will catch them. We just have to follow."

Eme ran without looking behind him. He could not believe that he had let Mbeku persuade him to do this. Of course they would get caught, and now they were going to die without anyone knowing what happened to them.

"Faster, Eme, we have to get out of here," Mbeku urged.

"I'm doing my best," Eme panted.

Their quarrel was cut short by voices.

"Little bell! Little bell, where are you?" Aku's voice called out.

Mbeku had a bad feeling. Then he heard a ringing sound start to emanate from his stomach. The tortoise thought fast. To the surprise of the goat, he hopped off Eme's back.

"What are you doing?" Eme tried not to screech, but he was not successful.

"Don't ask, just dig." Mbeku said, and he started to paw at the ground.

After a moment of hesitation, Eme followed suit. With his help, the process went much faster, and soon they had a big enough hole for Mbeku to cover his entire body. The tortoise kept digging.

They heard Aku's voice call out again. "Little bell, where are you? Little bell, ring for me!"

Mbeku heard another ring come from his stomach, and he picked up his pace in fright. The voice sounded closer. Soon the spirits would be able to hear the bell.

"Don't stop, Eme. We need to hide," Mbeku explained. "Their eyes are high up; maybe they won't see us."

Reinvigorated by his knowledge of the plan, Eme speeded up his work.

They heard Aka's voice this time. "Brother, are you sure we will be able to find it?"

"Yes, I'm sure, don't worry," Aku reassured his brother and called out for his bell again. This time he heard something. "Did you hear that? You see? We will find the thief."

The brothers eagerly walked toward the direction of the sound.

By this time, Mbeku and the goat had managed to dig a hole big enough for both of them. They hurried in and pulled the earth down to cover them. Eme realized that the tip of one of his horns was sticking out.

"Mbeku, we have a problem," Eme whispered, and explained the situation. By this time, they could feel the ground start to tremble from the spirits' approach.

"It's too late," Mbeku whispered back. "Try to be as still as possible. We have a chance."

The two friends stopped talking, and they heard Aku's voice call out again.

"Little bell, ring for me!"

Mbeku heard the ringing sound again, and this time, the spirits did too.

"It's close!" Aka exclaimed. "But where is it?"

The brothers wandered in circles, calling out for the bell and hearing it ring in response. They could not find where the sound was coming from.

"Maybe they aren't in this forest anymore." Aku mused. They were just about to give up when Aka tripped on Eme's horn.

"Eish! What is that?" The brothers knelt down and brought their eyes to the ground.

"Well, look here. I think we found our thief," Aku said in delight.

Eme felt a hand on his horn, and he stared wide-eyed at Mbeku, who stared back. He just had time to whisper, "Run, Mbeku!" before he was yanked out of the ground.

Mbeku choked back his scream as his friend was pulled out of the ground. The spirits did not bother looking further, convinced that they had found their thief.

"It's a little goat!" Aka said. "Brother, maybe this way we don't have to hunt tomorrow," he suggested.

Aku examined the goat before swinging him over his right shoulder. "Yes, we can rest tomorrow."

"Oh no, you don't want to eat me" Eme said, panicked. He was not expecting to be caught so easily. But at least Mbeku was not with him, he consoled himself. His friend would go free.

"We had something else to eat, but you ate that, so now we'll eat you." Aka talked like he was singing and not talking about ending Eme's life.

The goat shivered and tried to squirm free. Unfortunately, the spirits were too strong. They held Eme in place and headed back to their camp.

Mbeku waited for the spirits to walk away before climbing out of his hiding place. He followed after them from a safe distance by tracking their footprints in the ground. Unlike the spirits, whose eyes were to the sky, Mbeku could spot the trail they left behind with no problem.

When Mbeku arrived at the spirits' camp, they had Eme tied to a tree, and they were eating the rest of their food. The meat they had caught earlier was now roasting on the fire. Mbeku waited for the spirits to fall asleep before he carried out his plan. He sneaked over to the tree that held Eme and started to saw at it with a sharp rock.

Eme woke up suddenly when he felt the ropes that bound him move. The first thing he saw was Mbeku grinding a sharp rock against the ropes. Eme felt his heart warm. Once the first rope got loose, Eme had enough space to gnaw at the other ropes with his teeth. Together they got the rest of the ropes off. They turned to check on the spirits, but they were still asleep. With that confirmed, Mbeku and Eme sneaked back out of the spirit camp. Once they got far enough away, Mbeku climbed onto Eme's back once more, and they took off running.

Eme did not stop running until the spirit forest was replaced by the browns and greens that he was familiar with. Then he felt the tortoise fall off his side and they both collapsed on the forest floor. For a moment, there was just the sound of their heavy breathing, and then Eme started to laugh.

Mbeku joined in, and soon both friends were laughing too hard to breathe. Once they calmed down, they sat up and looked at each other.

"So," Eme said. "I have enough grass to last us until the rains come again."

Mbeku shook his head and started walking toward Eme's home. "That sounds like the best thing I've ever heard."

CHAPTER 9
UDENOLU

Once in a place called Amambi, a spirit was born as flesh. He was born on a night the sky swallowed the moon. The absence of the moon blurred the lines between the worlds of man and spirit, and as his body was forming, a spirit latched on to it, permanently changing him. Instead of carrying a human spirit, he was something else. He was brought into this world as neither man nor woman, alive nor dead. Humans tried to assign roles and fit him into their society, but he knew he did not fit. As he grew up, he stayed lost and confused. He did not farm, or tap wine, or start a trade. He talked of spirits and creatures invisible to everyone else. He was plagued by bad dreams, and he would sometimes wake his family with his screams. Because of this, most people called him strange because they did not understand him and he did not have a mind that pleased them. And they called him lazy because he did not contribute to the community. They did their best to avoid him.

His family called diviners to consult Chukwu, but the dibìàs always returned without answers. There was no agwu ailing him, so there was nothing to heal or fix. Eventually the dibìàs stopped coming. Before he left, the last dibìà gave a simple diagnosis—nsọ ani, a sin had led to his condition. The dibìà did not have proof, but he claimed that was the only option. His family left him alone after that. They provided shelter and food, but beyond that, no one knew what to do for him. He lived like this until he was the last member of his family in Amambi. His parents became ancestors, and his siblings married into different communities. The community members took on the role of caring for him. Even though they did not like him, they could not deny him life. Still, the people did not like that he was, in their opinion, refusing to participate in society. They started to call him Udenolu, after the vulture. To them, he was a scavenger, picking the meat off their work.

Udenolu was beautiful. His voice was like soft earth. His skin was a deep shade of the darkest brown, and it soaked in so much sun that it shined. But Udenolu hardly spoke. He did not adorn his skin with ùlì to show his beauty; he did not wrestle to show his strength or dance to show his grace. He did not show himself at all. He stayed away from everyone else and spent his time wandering or watching the sky. One day, while Udenolu was in an empty field of grass watching the sky, an old woman came up to him.

She looked like she had come from the market. She was wearing a long wrapper tied around her upper chest, and her neck was decorated with wooden beaded necklaces. She carried a large basket of produce on her head, and she sat it down next to him. "Udene."

He moved away. He did not understand what she wanted. "Are you talking to me?"

"Who else would I be talking to?" She bent and tapped the side of the basket. "Help me carry it. You see how old I am? At my age, how can I be carrying something so heavy on my own?"

Udenolu glanced at the basket again and realized that it *was* heavy and that she was old. He still felt reluctant to help. His reluctance felt like fear, and he realized that was because he was afraid. He did not understand why she wanted him, of all people, to help her.

Some of his fear must have shown, because her voice softened, and she said, "Come. I have no one at home to keep me company."

Udenolu nodded, but he could not bring himself to speak. He picked up the basket and followed behind the old woman as she led him to her home. They arrived at a house on the outskirts of Amambi. There were no compound walls. The house had a cooking station on the side, and farmland spread out behind it until it met a small clay fence that separated it from the forest. They entered the home, and Udenolu found himself in a large central room that led to two smaller rooms. He could not see into them because their entrances were closed off by curtains.

"You can set the basket down."

Udenolu did as she said, and then he separated the food into small piles for storage. He turned back to her to ask what else he could do, and he realized he did not know her name. "How do I call you?" His tone was shy. He knew they were from the same land, but he had never seen this woman before.

She was not hurt by him not knowing her name. She just smiled and said, "My name is too old now; everyone that knew it has returned to Ani. Just call me Nné." She eyed him up and down, and then added, "Have you eaten? Come."

She did not wait for an answer before she walked out, so Udenolu followed her to the cooking fire. Nné opened the still-warming pot and scooped the last of its contents into two small bowls. She set them on the ground, sat down, and gestured for Udenolu to sit across from her.

They ate in silence. Udenolu was surprised by how comfortable he was. He glanced at Nné every other moment, expecting something—he did not know what—but she just kept eating. She did not even look at him.

Udenolu cleared his throat and asked, "Why are you talking to me?" He did not know why she had brought him to her home or why she was treating him so differently from everyone else.

Nné paused her eating and looked up. "I was worried you would disappear."

"What?"

"Making yourself so small; I was worried you would disappear." She smiled. "We can't have that, can we?"

Udenolu did not respond, but each bite after that sparked a warm, tickling feeling in the base of his throat that spread out to warm the insides of his stomach. They did not speak until they were done eating.

"Tomorrow, you will help me on the farm," Nné said as she stood. "I will show you where you sleep."

Udenolu was sure he had not volunteered to work on her farm or sleep in her house, but he found himself nodding and following her to see the space. It was one of the smaller rooms in her house. Udenolu assumed that Nné slept in the other room. His room had a raffia mat and a covered pot that he discovered was filled with cool water.

Nné left to tend to her own matters and once he was left alone, Udenolu felt the sudden, desperate urge to run. His feet were moving before he could question the urge, but he held back from breaking into a full run and took quick strides instead. He walked out of his room and then the house.

Daylight was starting to fade, but Udenolu had never been scared of the dark. He decided to circle the land around the house—the movement would help him think.

As he walked, he thought about the unfamiliar, full feeling he had. It was not as if he had not been full before, but something felt different this time. Warmer. Maybe it was worth it to stay.

When he returned to Nné's house, she was already asleep. He made his way to his room, taking care to make as little noise as possible. Once he made it into his room, he lay down and went to sleep, telling himself he didn't have to stay if he didn't want to, even though he knew he wouldn't be leaving. Udenolu's sleep that night was restless. He dreamt he had wings, made of beautiful eagle feathers, that grew out of his back. He tried to fly as high as he could, but the ground was pulling him down. He plunged into deep crevices in soil that seemed depthless. In his dream, his body twitched as he twisted through endless space, only just missing outcroppings of rock and clay. He felt something calling to him. He could reach it; he knew he could...

Udenolu opened his eyes. A stillness entered his body that made its earlier restlessness seem false. He took a short moment to collect himself before he got ready for the day.

It was still dark when he stepped outside, but hints of light were beginning to peek through from under the shadow of night. Nné wasn't awake, so Udenolu decided to make the morning meal. He started a cooking fire and put water in a large pot to boil. Then he gathered the ingredients to make okpa. As the water boiled, he opened a bag of okpa flour and scooped out enough for him and Nné into a small mixing pot. He added salt to the flour, and then palm oil and mixed the ingredients together until the flour took on a bright yellow color.

Udene stood and stretched his limbs. Daylight had spread across the sky, but it did not have the harsh sting of true morning. By now the water was warm, so Udene removed some water and poured it into a shallower pot. He added some more salt to the water and used the warm water to wash some dried banana leaves. When he was done, he rolled the leaves into small cones and tied them with raffia twine. Then he brought his mixing bowl close to the fire and added water to the flour mixture until it turned into a paste that he smoothed out with a wooden spoon. He added more water until the paste became liquid. He scooped the food into the banana leaves and tied their openings shut. He made four in total and placed them into the cooking pot over a layer of leaves.

Udenolu washed his hands and cleaned up. He was about to start sweeping the area around the house when he heard Nné's voice from inside the house.

"Udene, have you woken up?" The sound of her footsteps drew near as she left the house.

"Eehay, do I smell okpa? Fresh okpa?" She sounded delighted and her steps quickened. "Okpa di oku?"

Udenolu laughed, catching himself off guard. "Nné, did you sleep well? Yes, hot okpa. It will be ready soon."

"I slept so well. I'm ready to eat this early," she said as she came into view. She stopped before reaching Udenolu and squinted at his face.

"How about you? I think I heard you last night. What was disturbing your sleep?"

Udenolu looked away and stared at the ground. "Bad dreams." He shrugged and then sank to the floor, choosing to sit with his legs pulled up against his chest. Nné came to sit next to him.

"What do you dream of?"

"Flying."

"Flying?"

"Yes, the..." Udenolu stopped himself. He was going to talk about the feeling of flying through the sky, but that was not what he had dreamt about. His dreams took him downward.

"I dream of falling," he said instead.

"Are you scared to fall?"

Udenolu was surprised. When people asked about his dreams, they wanted to stop them or figure them out. That was not what was happening now. He had not thought about how he felt about his dreams while he was in them. He always woke up feeling sad, or frustrated, or ashamed, because he knew he was doing something that he was not meant to do. That was why he wanted the dreams to stop; that was why they were bad. But, was he scared to fall while he was dreaming?

He shook his head. "No, I'm not scared."

Nné clicked her tongue. "You know, falling and flying are often the same thing, but there's a significant difference."

"What is it?"

"Flying is reaching for something. Falling is acceptance." She chuckled, and Udenolu watched the beads across her neck shake from the tremble of her shoulders.

"For both of those things, what's most important is that you have wings."

Udenolu twisted his neck to look behind him, almost expecting to see a new feathery limb growing out of his back. There was nothing.

He felt Nné's hand cup his cheeks; then she turned his head and pressed her lips to his forehead. She held the moment before letting go.

"The okpa should be ready now. Go and bring me some."

Udenolu walked to the cooking pot and opened it up, inhaling the smoke and the smell of good food. He pulled out the wraps by the strings, wincing when the heat stung his fingers.

"You can use a spoon!" Nné suggested.

"No, I'm fine." Udenolu came back with the plate and before he sat down placed it in front of Nné. "Let's eat?" He waited for Nné to pick up a serving before he joined her.

Their silent meal was interrupted by a group of hunters walking past Udenolu and Nné toward the forest.

"Aah, Nné, is everything alright?" One of the members of the group, a tall, stocky woman, stopped walking and looked between Udenolu and Nné. Her three companions stopped when they noticed she was not with them and headed back to her.

Udenolu felt a tightness in his chest and his throat constricting his breath. Tears stung his eyes, and he did not know if he was upset or angry. He wanted to be left alone.

"Is the scavenger taking from you?" said the tall woman.

"Tell us, and we can see him off," said another hunter—a tall, slender man carrying a bow.

Nné looked at Udenolu, who was glaring at the hunters, and then she stood to address the cocky group.

"Do you have to show off?"

"What?" The hunters exchanged glances, looks of confusion lining their faces.

"Do you have to show off your foolishness?" said Nné, clarifying her question. "You see that we are sitting here, eating in peace, and yet you came to disturb it. Did they send you?" When she said "they," she tilted her head in the direction of the forest to indicate spirits.

"Ah..." The hunters fidgeted—this was not the conversation they had planned on having.

The two hunters who had not spoken grabbed their companions' hands and started walking in the direction of the forest. They did not get far before the woman who had started the conversation ran back. Before she spoke, she looked at Nné and then at Udenolu, who was still glaring at her. Her voice was measured despite her nervous appearance.

"Nné. I shouldn't have said that. You're right. It was foolishness." She stared at Udenolu again before she added, "I'm sorry. You didn't do anything to me. I have no right to quarrel with you." She nodded once before returning to the other hunters.

Udenolu and Nné watched the group leave, and then they exchanged glances and laughed.

Nné clapped her hands. "Okay, we have fed our bellies. Now we feed the land."

She took Udenolu to the farmland behind her house. She was growing rows of cocoyams that had long, broad, green leaves. She showed Udenolu how to care for her farm; to weed the plants, and to check the soil for dryness. She explained how to pull out the plants when they were ready, and how to store them. That day started a new cycle in Udenolu's life. He would wake up, cook, clean, and eat with Nné. When he was done, they would tend to the farm, or she would send him to the market. At night, when the business of day settled, she would ask him questions.

"Did you dream again?" "Where do you go when you dream?" "Are you alone in your dreams?"

Udenolu found that with each conversation, the boundaries grew thin between his dream world and the world he lived in. He had been pushing down his dreams, moving them to the furthest corners of his mind where awareness could not reach. He could not do that with Nné. She pulled him out with her questions.

As time passed, he noticed the wrinkles on Nné's face deepen. Her hair, which had been flecked with gray strands when he met her, became more gray than black. She grew distracted, often turning her head to respond to a voice he could not hear. With age, she grew closer to the world of spirits, and Ani was calling her.

One night during their talks, she asked a new question.

"Do you know why the vulture is Ani's messenger?"

Udenolu shook his head. They were outside their shared house, sitting across from each other. Their faces were illuminated by the small fire between them. The light played with the shadows, extending and shrinking them as it saw fit. Nné smiled. Her back was to the night, making her seem hidden, except for her smile. When she spoke, the voice came from the darkness behind her.

"There is a reason we let the vulture eat sacrifices. When it hunts, it claws the meat off dead animals, turning death into life. The vulture is a messenger of Ani, and just like the python, it exists between this world and the next."

Nné cleared her throat. "They called you a scavenger?" She laughed. "They were right, and they didn't even understand what they were saying. Scavengers live off death; for Ani, life and death are the same thing. There is no separation in her, just as there is no separation in you."

She stopped speaking, but Udenolu still heard her words. When it came out, his voice was hoarse and trembling. "How do you know? I mean, how are you sure? What if you're wrong?"

Nné leaned forward. Her eyebrows were drawn into sharp lines, but her words softened them.

"Udene, you listen to me. I see you. You are known. That's not the problem. You do not need to be seen. You need to see yourself. Know yourself."

She stood up and patted his shoulder before walking into the house. Udenolu did not say anything; by now, he was used to her abrupt ways of coming and going. He focused on what she said, repeating it in his mind. "You need to see yourself." I need to see myself? He frowned. Who was he? Udenolu stayed awake late into the night, until he could not see his hand in front of his face, even with the light. He put out the fire and went to bed.

That night, Udenolu shifted. Usually when he dreamt, his body would transform itself and give him the capacity to fly across mountains and fields of grass that he had never seen. This time he was a bird. A vulture. He had deep brown feathers and a white fleck on his back, which represented death and the spirit realm. He was also still in Amambi. He stood on a tall tree, right at the edge of the forest. He flew around Amambi several times to learn about his new body. Was this who he was? Why? He was flying over one of the altars to Ani when a dibìà walked out. His face was half covered with chalk, and he raised his ọfọ at Udenolu.

"You! Who are you? Say your name!"

Udenolu did not know how to talk, so he turned around despite the calls of the dibìà and returned to the forest. He stayed on the tree until light broke through in the sky. Then he blinked, and he was waking up in his human body. Someone, Nné, was calling his name.

"Udene! The dibìà is here for you."

Udenolu felt a stab of fear, but he had not done anything wrong, so he walked out with his head held straight. The dibìà was the same one as last night's. Nné had found a wooden stool—he did not know from where—so the dibìà was sitting comfortably in their central room. When he saw Udenolu walk out, he stood.

"Did you rise well?" He was staring intently at Udenolu, as if every word that came out of his mouth next would be crucial.

"Yes, I'm awake. Thank you." Udenolu kept his response short. He did not know what was happening. Nné walked in with a bowl of kola and another stool, but this one was more like a log. She nodded at them and patted Udenolu on the back before leaving. He did not know if she had really said it, but as she left, he heard, "Know yourself."

The dibìà eyed him, and then he shook his head and slumped. "I should have known."

"What?"

The dibìà looked back up. He stared at Udenolu's face as if it were hurting him. "I should have known. The signs are all there. Even your face is a spirit face." He collected himself and continued talking. "I am sorry, Udenolu. I'm sorry. The whole of Amambi owes you an apology. It is us who have done the great sin—to see spirit and not recognize it."

Udenolu's eyes widened. His mind raced to figure out what the dibìà was telling him, but he could not get far before the dibìà spoke again.

"Call your bird."

Udenolu shook his head. "I don't know how."

The dibìà laughed. "This is the first thing that you will learn. You do know; the practice is learning to be aware of what you know."

"I'm learning?"

"Yes, of course." The dibìà smacked his thigh. "I did not mention that. You are not human, not entirely. You should know that now, yes?"

Udenolu nodded again, starting to feel like a lizard. "Yes, I know. A dibìà we called said I am this way because someone had offended Anị, but he did not know what to do to heal it."

The dibìà shook his head. "Yes, I know. I was one of the ones your family called. You won't remember me; I was called in your first seasons. You would cry so loudly at night that your compound could not sleep." He chuckled. "I felt the death touch on you even then. Something not from here. When I learned you were told you were nsọ, I thought it made sense. Maybe someone in your family had offended or created a spirit that latched on to you during your passage to this realm." He tutted. "I was foolish."

"You were?"

The dibìà laughed. "Will you just be repeating my words?"

Udenolu responded, "Well, I, no. I don't think so."

"I'm joking," the dibìà said, laughing. "Yes, I was foolish. We all were, because your face carries life just as strongly as death."

The dibìà spent more time explaining the mysteries of spirits, but Udenolu couldn't concentrate on any of it. Udenolu knew he would be taught again, so he listened in silence, making note of what he didn't understand. When the dibìà left, it was with promises to return soon. He kept his word. The next day he showed up to take Udenolu and Nné to a community meeting. Udenolu was nervous. It had been a long while since he had felt safe enough to be in large groups. He looked at Nné, who was standing resolutely beside him, and he made up his mind.

"Let's go."

The meeting was not what he expected. First, before he could even arrive, he could hear music. Drums, flutes, and other sounds blended into a high-tempo rhythm that quickened his blood. When he came into view, the crowd grew silent. Then the oldest person in the crowd, a titled elder named Maduga, stood to speak.

"Ude... ah." He stopped, remembering that the name the town gave Udenolu was in jest.

Udenolu understood his hesitancy, so he clarified, "It's okay. I like the name. It's a true one."

Ọzo Maduga accepted Udenolu's permission and continued. "Yes, Udenolu, we don't know what to say to you." He gestured at the crowd around him. "We rejected you. We judged you. We did not treat you like kin umunna. You are one of ours, and we failed in our responsibilities to you. In doing so, we have offended Anị. We are sorry."

The rest of the crowd murmured assent, and Udenolu could make out short sentences like "yes, that's the truth" and "it's a disgrace." He hung his head and fell deep into thought. The people allowed him his time. It was not their place to rush him.

Finally, he said, "Let's talk."

Then something beautiful took place in Amambi's community square. The people and Udenolu took turns sharing their experiences. Udenolu would mention something someone had said or done that rested on his heart, and the person would come up to account for it. Through this, he learned stories of people's moments of anger, their shame, their pain. There was always something that made it easy to excuse hurting him. After the stories ended, he spoke again.

"You know, what you are all telling me is that you're scared. You are scared of being scared. Of danger. So anytime you meet something that might be different or unusual, you treat it like a threat. I just happened to be the most different."

The people murmured words of assent. They felt the truth of his words.

Udenolu continued. "You aren't wrong. Life is dangerous. I am dangerous." He paused to look at the people staring back at him. "But so are you. Remember that."

He stood and the people's eyes followed him. He stared at the different faces in the crowd one more time, before nodding. "Okay, I have heard you. I accept your gifts."

The crowd broke out into laughter and cheers, and a few people even ran up to him, clasping him on the back or hugging him where they could reach. He heard shouts of "Ézè Anị" through the crowd. Once their excitement died down, the music started back up, and this time there was food. Udenolu sat with the rest of his community and enjoyed their warmth for the first time.

After that day, Udenolu started to learn with the dibìàs. He went through training and initiations that allowed him to see through the material world, into the spirit realm, even in his human body. At night he would fly around Amambi, protecting it from malicious spirits. As he grew closer to Anị, he started to bring messages to the people—of harvest or war, as Anị told him. His competence and his heart led to the songwriters making music in his name. At the end of his training, he took on the title of Ézè Anị, as a priest of Anị, the first in Amambi. Nné was at the ceremony, and she smiled wider than everyone in town combined.

One day, months after receiving his title, Udenolu went to visit Nné, but he found her still sleeping, unable to wake up. Her body did not house her spirit anymore. When Udenolu found her, he informed her family and the members of Amambi. As the closest living person to her, Udenolu was responsible for her burial. He cried with the dibìàs who had come to support him while Nné's body was lowered into the ground and covered with earth. He knew that the world did not belong to humans permanently, and any time in this realm was a gift. He knew that her soul had gone onto the next stage of her journey. Yet when he realized he would no longer have conversations by the fire, or work in the garden, or anything else with her, he cried. The tears could not stop, and he did not want them to.

His tears contained all the love she had given him, and so he kept crying while the dibìàs held him.

After Nné's body was returned to the earth, the people of Amambi prepared to send off her spirit to the ancestral realm. Even though she had no living relatives, her send-off was one of the biggest that Amambi had ever seen. People showed up with gifts of cowry and precious stones to send her off. Even one of the famous Oka blacksmiths, the best in Igboland, presented a present—a bronze statue of a vulture.

The people of Amambi ate, played music, danced, and told stories of Nné. At the center of it all was Udenolu. As Ézè Anị, he presided over the ceremony, sometimes sharing stories of Nné that no one else knew.

While he talked with the people, he did not tell them that the spirits had come to join them. Attracted by their merriment and the recent death, wandering spirits filled the cleared-off space. He noticed when Nné arrived. She danced with the dancers, ate food from the tables of others, and she did it all while laughing. Out of the corner of his eyes, he saw the ground open up. He heard voices and laughter. If he focused, he could even smell food and wine. The elders in the spirit world had heard their celebrations, and they were preparing for a new ancestor. Nné turned to smile at him. He knew she had seen him all along. Then she fell, returning to the world of spirits.

The ground closed and no one seemed to have noticed. Udenolu stared at the space that had been a portal to the spirit realm just a moment ago. He thought of Nné. When she fell, it looked like she was flying.

CHAPTER 10
THE TORTOISE AND THE LION KING

In the middle of the grasslands of the animal kingdom were the lion caves. From a distance, they looked like three giant disks of rock stacked on one another. Somehow these rocks had grown together, forming a semi-hollow, curving spiral. The entrance to the cave was split ever so often with a thick slab of rock. The cave ended up looking like a tense, curled-up snake with its mouth open and ready to pounce. The ground around the cave was made of the same red-brown earth as the cave, but it eventually gave way to green grasslands. Low-lying trees with spread-out branches graced the landscape.

The lion king, Ibem, paced the extravagant cave that was his throne room. At the back of the room, carved out of the center of the wall, was a throne fit for a lion. Legend had it that the very first lion king, Odum, carved out the throne himself. Now it served as the throne for all kings after him. King Ibem stopped moving to look at the low, flat slab of rock, covered in hide and cloth, that was his throne. He had faced a lot of challenges in his life. Persuading different tribes of animals to work together was no small feat, and he liked to think he had done a good job. His time as king had strengthened his character and determination. Who would have thought that both would be tested by his own child?

As if summoned by his thoughts, the girl in question walked into his chambers.

"I was told you wanted to speak with me?" The young lioness entered the throne room with more ease than even the strongest warriors in the kingdom. Ibem turned to greet his daughter.

"Anuli, you're here. Have you given any more thought to your marriage?"

"Have you given any more thought to my idea?" came the quick retort. Ibem was not having it.

"I never agreed to your plan. You know that." Ibem walked away from his daughter and toward his throne. Then he sat, facing her. "Who picks their marriage from a competition?"

"I do." Anuli faced her father with her head held high. She would not back down. "Who wants to get married to the children of their father's friends?" She made a gagging sound as if she were spitting up a hairball. In fact, she was sure she felt a few strands of hair on her tongue.

"Your sister had no problem settling down," Ibem said. His ears twitched and his eyes held a spark of amusement, but he gave no verbal indicator that he was amused by his daughter's actions. "Is it possible that you just don't want to get married?

If that's the case, let me know and we can revisit it some other time."

His daughter shook her head and groaned. "No, that isn't it." She sat back on her hind legs. "My sister had no problem getting married, because she's just like them. Very, very smart." Anuli paused for effect. "And very, very boring." She slumped her shoulders. "So boring. The most boring. I can't do that for the rest of my life. Please." She let her forelegs drop as well and tried to convey how desperately she wanted this. "Pleeaaaaase."

Ibem hesitated. "It's risky to open up a tournament to everyone. What if someone horrible wins? They get access to half the kingdom through you. It could be dangerous."

Anuli bounced up and went toward her father. "They won't, I promise. How about I pick three animals out of whoever arrives? The competition can just be between them." She turned up her nose and preened. "I'm a good judge of character, you know."

Ibem was not convinced, but he doted on his daughters, so he agreed. "Okay, let's do as you wish. I'll ask the birds and squirrels to spread the news around the animal kingdom. In twelve days, we will hold a competition to choose your spouse—oompfh." Ibem staggered as his daughter flung herself at him, nearly knocking him off his throne.

"Thank you! This is going to be amazing!" Anuli ran out of the room before her father could say anything in response.

Ibem managed to collect himself, and then he looked down at his throne. "Well, it might not be the worst thing to happen. Sometimes change is good, hopefully."

The rhino guards outside the throne room exchanged glances but did not say a word. It seemed like their king was having a hard time.

Days later, the tortoise was returning to his home when his path was blocked by a crowd of animals. The way ahead cut through a winding river and Mbeku did not want to go for an unexpected swim, so he twisted his body to move through the forest of limbs and wings.

"Mbeku, is that you?" Okpoko, the bird, stretched her neck to get a better glimpse of the tortoise through the crowd.

Mbeku did not want to stop walking and risk being crushed, so he pushed through the crowd before turning to find the source of the voice. Spotting the hornbill, he circled the edge of the crowd toward her direction. The bird followed suit and fought her way through the crowd. They moved away from the crowd to talk.

"Have you heard the news?" The bird did not wait for a response before she said, "The king's second daughter is getting married! Anuli!"

The tortoise blinked at his friend and turned to leave, but he stopped at her next words.

"She says she's going to hold a competition and marry the winner!"

"A competition?"

Seeing that she had his attention, the bird nodded vigorously and further explained, "Yes. We didn't receive any information about the competition itself, but we know the rewards. Whoever Anuli chooses shares her roles and status in the lion kingdom. Isn't that half the lion kingdom? They would never want for anything again." Okpoko sighed, the wistful note clear in her voice. "Of course, all of the animal kingdom will want to compete in something like that. It's for the strongest and bravest, not for regular animals like us."

Mbeku did not respond. His mind was churning. "Okpoko, when is the competition?"

The bird was taken aback. "Eight days, why?" She jumped slightly off the ground. "Mbeku, you couldn't possibly be thinking of going?"

"Why not?"

Okpoko tried to reason with Mbeku. "Do you know the kinds of animals who would show up to such a thing? Wolves! Foxes! Jaguars!" Her voice was a high-pitched shrill by the time she finished talking, but Mbeku just shook his head.

"How will I know if I don't do it? Before someone else tells me no, should I tell myself no? Of course not. I can, at least, find out what the competition is first, and then I can decide how to continue."

"You're really going to go?"

Mbeku thought of his past. Sometimes being a tortoise was not easy. If he found a home, but another animal wanted it, he had to move. There were few people he could fight, so he had to use his brains. But maybe, if he were married to the daughter of the lion king, it would not have to be that way. As for leading the kingdom, well, maybe he could ask for an exemption. He made up his mind.

"Yes, I'm really going to go."

The crowd outside the lion caves was massive. Usually the land around their territory would be void of almost all animals but the lions. Now there was no room to stand. Ibem and his family were the main ones to use the caves. The other lions preferred to live in the seemingly endless plain of grasslands that surrounded the caves. Anuli peeked out at the crowd from behind a cave wall, and her eyes widened in surprise. How was she meant to select from all these animals? There was every kind of animal, from the proud bulls with long tusks to gobbling turkeys, and there were even a few scorpions. She shook her head and retreated to the cave, saying a quick thanks to her former self for agreeing to choose only three animals to compete. She could not imagine having to handle this crowd.

Down in the crowd, Mbeku tried to stay out of the way of the other animals. They all seemed interested in showing off their prowess. He wondered how all these animals could possibly compete. Once his thoughts got that far, his eyes lit up and he stealthily made his way to the front of the crowd. He had a feeling they were not *all* going to compete.

"Thank you all for coming!"

A hush descended over the crowd after the lion king spoke. The animals turned their gazes to the caves, and the lion came out of the central door, with his daughter beside him. He turned to his right and addressed Anuli, but those at the front of the crowd could make out his words.

"Okay, Anuli, you can handle it from here?" He said it like a question, so his daughter nodded.

Anuli stepped forward and addressed the crowd. "Thank you for coming. I don't want to keep you waiting for longer than you have been already. I'm sure your journeys here were not easy." She paused and looked out at the crowd. Each animal that met her gaze responded almost automatically. They straightened their postures and raised their heads. Some of them even adopted haughty smiles. Then Anuli noticed a small tortoise at the front of the crowd. Unlike the others, he met her gaze calmly. They looked at each other for a moment and Anuli's eyes glistened with interest. Then she looked away and the moment passed, like a memory of a dream. She continued her address.

"For this competition, I will be choosing three animals from the crowd to compete."

The animals broke out into discussions about her words. Some of them were angry, thinking they had been deceived into believing they had a chance. Others were even more sure of themselves, recalling Anuli looking at them earlier. The tortoise felt a sense of excitement build. He had guessed something like this might happen, so he moved to the front, but he had not expected the number of people competing to be so small. His excitement turned to nerves at the thought that he might not be chosen. He tried to remind himself that nothing had been decided yet.

"I understand that you might be upset, but I invite you to stay for the competition. We will, of course, be housing and feeding you for the entire event. I will make my selections today, and it will take place tomorrow," Anuli explained.

The animals were slightly mollified, and they started to anticipate a fun event. Some were betting on getting picked. Anuli smiled at their regained enthusiasm and prepared to make her selection. Sensing the change in her mood, the animals turned somber. Some sneaked glances at the other animals around them, wondering who would be picked.

Anuli stepped into the crowd, and the crowd reflexively parted around her. She walked up to a black leopard that was standing in the crowd. When she looked at him, he had not tried to make himself something he was not, like the others. There was no haughty smile or false confidence. Instead, the leopard smiled at her, almost instinctively, before he caught himself and ducked his head. She liked him.

"What's your name?"

He rushed out a response. "Kalu. My name is Kalu."

"Kalu," Anuli repeated. "You're my first choice." She smiled at the startled leopard and gestured with her head. "You can go stand next to my father. I need two more people." Kalu swallowed air and went to stand as close to the king as he dared, which meant he left enough space to fit an elephant between them.

Anuli kept moving through the crowd. The next time she stopped in front of a speckled hyena. Without prompting, he started speaking.

"My name is Adim. Thank you for the opportunity to..." He was cut off by Anuli's laughter.

"I like you, Adim." Her voice was warm with delight, and she gestured for him to join Kalu. She had noticed Adim in the crowd because he could not stay still. Every part of his body seemed to vibrate with constant excitement. She figured he would not be boring. Leading the animals was hard, important work, but she wanted to be able to have fun when she needed it. Adim seemed to share her need for excitement, except maybe he was excited. She laughed to herself, then returned her attention to her current task. It was time to pick her last competitor.

Anuli turned and walked back toward the front of the crowd. The disappointment on the faces of the animals in the back was visible. However, a lot of the animals in the front were not too hopeful. What were the chances that they would be the last one chosen? Meanwhile, the tortoise felt the dwindling embers of his hope reignite. When Anuli had chosen the leopard, then the hyena, he had thought he had no chance, but just maybe...

"You're my final choice." Anuli's voice interrupted Mbeku's train of thought, and before he could make sense of it, he heard the other animals begin to react.

"Really, she chose the tortoise?"

"Him?"

"I understand losing to a leopard, but Mbeku?"

Some of the animals grumbled in dissatisfaction, but Mbeku did not care. The other animals might not think he was deserving, but it was not their choice to make. Then he saw the look on the king's face and his heart sank. The king could not look any more displeased. Naysayers were one thing, but would Anuli really choose him when her own father clearly did not like him? With his head hanging low, Mbeku walked to stand next to Kalu and Adim. Following Kalu's lead, the three of them stood a distance away from the king. While the lion was neutral toward the other contestants, he was concerned about Mbeku, who was known to be a trickster.

With her selection made, Anuli returned to her father's side and addressed the crowd. "Thank you for coming, again. We will meet at first light tomorrow for the competition."

The animals wandered off, some to inspect their surroundings and others to settle down for the day. Anuli turned to look at the three competitors. The tortoise met her gaze, calm as usual, Adim perked up at her glance, and the leopard did not meet her eyes.

"Okay, the three of you can stay in the inner caves. Make sure to get some rest tonight." She suddenly was not sure what to say to them. She said a quick good-bye and left with her father. The three animals looked at each other and shrugged, and then followed the lions in. Once they entered, they were met by other lions, who showed them where they would be sleeping.

Later that night, Ibem and his daughter were in the midst of another disagreement. This time they were in Anuli's room. The father and daughter stood across from each other, their words coming out in low rumbles.

"I don't think it's fair to assume he's planning something," Anuli argued. She felt like her father was judging the tortoise too harshly.

"I think it would be foolish to ignore who the tortoise is" was her father's quick response.

"Okay, you're right. He probably has a plan, but we don't know what it is."

"It's because we don't know what it is that I'm afraid," Ibem sighed. "Anything could happen."

"Exactly!" Anuli agreed. "Anything could happen, but you've lived long years, so what you're afraid of seems like the most possible thing. We have to remember we don't lead with fear."

Ibem stopped talking and thought through what his daughter had said before responding, "You're right. I am scared. I don't think I should ignore that, but I don't know what's happening. It isn't right to act like I do." He did not hide the pride in his voice when he told Anuli: "You've grown."

Happy to have gotten her father's understanding, Anuli left feeling lighter. Ibem, however, could not shake off his fear. He hoped his daughter was right, and he was not about to fall into one of Mbeku's schemes.

The next day the animals gathered on the grasslands outside the cave, their faces marked with astonishment. The area had been transformed overnight. Now there were small circles of food, water, and wine equally spaced apart. The left half of the rocky entrance to the caves was taken up by two slabs of rock formed into tables and laid vertically across. In groups, the animals gathered around the servings of food, but no one touched the meal since Anuli had not arrived. The animals did not have to wait too long before the lions came out, this time accompanied by the three competitors.

Anuli walked forward to address the gathered crowd. "I'm glad to see you all here. The competition will be simple." At the mention of the competition, all the animals, including the three competitors, perked up. This was the moment they were waiting for. Anuli then said, "I've had our cooks prepare the spiciest pepper soup. Your task is to finish it without pausing. The first person to do so wins."

Some of the animals breathed sighs of relief that they had not been chosen, while others grumbled because they believed that their spice tolerance could handle anything. Adim looked a little disappointed. He had been expecting something more challenging, but he cheered himself up. At least he would get free food. Adim's thoughts were interrupted when a group of bats flew out of the caves. They carried three gourds of soup between them and swiftly set them down in a row at the center of the exposed rock outside the cave entrance. This way the competitors would be in view of everyone in the crowd. Anuli directed Mbeku to the left, Adim to the center, and Kalu to the right. She addressed the crowd again.

"You are free to start eating." She paused for the crowds to settle into their meal. While she waited, she walked over to one of the stone slabs and lay down, her tail making lazy swings beside her. King Ibem followed her actions and took his place at the other seat. Anuli waited for the noise from the crowd to die down, and then, without bothering to leave her seat, she addressed the competitors.

"Your task is to finish the bowl of pepper soup in front of you. It should be cool enough to eat by now. Once you start moving your mouth, you cannot stop. The first person to finish—or whoever can finish the most—wins. Questions?" The three animals shook their heads. Kalu looked concerned, but Mbeku had a glint in his eyes. He had a plan.

"Okay." Anuli stood on her makeshift throne and growled. "Begin!"

Kalu dived straight into his bowl, his muzzle almost knocking over his food with the force he used. Wincing from the sting of the tiny bit of soup he got up his nose, Kalu moved his face away from the bowl but kept eating without sparing a glance at his competitors.

Adim and Mbeku started eating simultaneously. Adim took slow bites, taking time to chew and swallow the food. It seemed he was more interested in eating than competing. Mbeku ate quickly, but his speed did not rival Kalu's. The crowd and the lion judges were certain they already knew who would win. The competitors kept going at their bowls, but when Kalu was almost through, he choked and retreated from his bowl, with tears running down his eyes.

"Too hot!" Kalu gasped. He was done.

Neither Adim nor Mbeku had finished as much as Kalu. Only a few mouthfuls were left in Kalu's bowl, and as long as the other competitors stopped eating before they had eaten more than he had, he would win.

The excitement of the crowd rose at the unexpected upset. Their gaze turned to Adim, who was steadily making his way through the meal. He noted the eyes on him, and to the shock of the crowd, he retreated from his bowl, sat back on his hind legs, and proceeded to clean himself. His bowl had a little under half of the soup left. He had not eaten as much as Kalu. The gaze of the crowd turned to Mbeku.

The tortoise had eaten a bit faster than, Adim but not by much. The crowd could also see his nose begin to run. He was visibly near his spice-tolerance limit, so they knew he would give out soon.

Mbeku saw that Adim had ended the competition, and he knew it was time to start his plan. He took another mouthful of the soup and then began to talk. "You know, I really didn't think I had a chance."

The animals in the crowd looked at each other, and the king's ears twitched. He knew things had gone too smoothly.

The tortoise ignored the reactions of his audience and took another mouthful before continuing. "But now I might actually have a chance!" He paused to eat. Kalu zeroed in on the tortoise and frowned. Something about what he was doing did not seem quite right. Adim looked on with a wide grin, his tongue hanging out. Finally, some excitement.

"I'm the kind of tortoise that follows the rules, so if you say, 'I can't stop moving my mouth', I won't." Mbeku ended his declaration with a sense of self-righteousness before diving back into his bowl.

King Ibem could feel his blood boil at the audacity of the tortoise, but he reminded himself that this was not his event—it was his daughter's. He turned to Anuli and said, "You can end the competition now. You don't need to deal with this."

Anuli spared a distracted glance at her father before returning to look at the tortoise. She did not turn her head again, but she asked, "Why would I end the competition?"

King Ibem huffed. "Well, the tortoise. He's clearly cheating. He's using the breaks to cool down his tongue, so he can keep eating."

Anuli laughed. "I did say that their mouths shouldn't stop moving; he's not wrong. He's within the rules."

"I knew he was going to do something like this. Anuli, you cannot reward his scheming."

"Why not? I'm amused." The lioness laughed and nudged her distressed father with her head. "I don't know what decision I'm making yet, but I want to have fun. I'll ask questions later."

Ibem was concerned. His daughter thought she had reassured him, but she had just confirmed that the tortoise might be a choice. Yet he wanted to respect his daughter's decisions. It made no sense to allow her to make a choice and then make it for her.

"Okay, I'll listen to you, but be careful with that tortoise."

The tortoise was in the middle of another monologue. He alternated between talking and eating. He talked about the flavor of the food, the spice, and, repeatedly, the fact that he was doing what he was supposed to. His mouth never stopped moving. Eventually he ran out of food. He smiled to himself and looked around at the faces of his audience. They ranged from angry, to shocked, to impressed. Mbeku looked at the lions and waited to see what their decision would be.

Anuli spoke up when she saw that Mbeku had finished the soup. "Wow. I didn't think you would finish the whole thing, but I hoped you would." She addressed the three competitors. "I have questions for each of you. Who wants to go first?"

Adim raised his head to draw attention to himself, and Anuli nodded at him.

"Okay, Adim. Why did you come here? Why did you want to compete?"

The hyena looked away from Anuli; he seemed embarrassed. "Well, I didn't have much of a motivation really."

Anuli tilted her head and considered his answer. She was not sure if she should be offended or not. "I was hoping the person that chose to marry me would at least have some reason."

Adim winced when he realized his words sounded careless, and he clarified them. "I didn't think I could actually win. I just wanted something to do. Even during the competition, I wasn't really trying to win."

"That's true," Anuli agreed. "I don't have any more questions for you. I don't think your answers would matter either way, would they?"

Adim shook his head. "No, sorry. I'm not interested in getting married."

Anuli laughed to herself. She appreciated Adim's honesty. She chose the next competitor this time, instead of asking who wanted to be the next one questioned.

"Kalu, I have two questions."

The leopard started at the mention of his name, and he settled into an alert stance. "Yes, I'm ready."

"The first question is the same. Why are you here?"

Kalu had expected the question, so his answer was quick. "I wanted to prove myself." Anuli gestured for him to continue, and he did. "I'm not the most adventurous leopard. At home, everyone has done something. I knew of you, Anuli. You're known to be smart and strong and adventurous. I thought if I could be the kind of person that was worthy of you, then I would be the kind of person I wanted to be." The words came out of him in a rush and he immediately looked down.

Anuli liked the leopard, but she was not sure how she felt about being a test. "You think highly of me" was all she said before proceeding to her next question. "If you win, you will be responsible for leading half of the kingdom. Do you think you can do that?"

Kalu gave a prompt response again. "I think I can learn. I'm willing to work hard." Kalu was not sure if his answers were the right ones, but he knew they were true. The last competitor to be questioned was the tortoise. He geared himself up to answer the same questions, but Anuli surprised him.

"So why was your strategy cheating?"

Mbeku was nervous. He had not expected to get this far, and he said just that. "I thought I was going to lose; then I saw a chance, so I took it. I wanted to win."

"Why?" Surprisingly, this question came from Ibem. Anuli looked at him in surprise, but she gestured for Mbeku to answer.

Mbeku glanced at the crowd, and he recognized some of the faces staring at him. "I don't know if you know, but things don't always go smoothly for me. You're strong. I mean, you're lions. I thought that if I won, I would be safe. You mentioned leading the kingdom. I can help. I'm good at figuring things out."

"Okay, I've made my choice," Anuli said suddenly, bringing an end to the questions. "Mbeku, your strategy might be considered cheating by a lot of animals." She grinned, which on her looked more like baring her teeth. "But I'm the one who gets to decide, and I think it was funny and smart. Congratulations."

Mbeku stood stunned and unsure what that meant until Anuli clarified.

"You won."

"I won?"

"Yes, but..."

At Anuli's addition, Mbeku let his heart sink. He should have known there would be a problem.

"I don't want to marry you."

"Oh." Mbeku paused. Well, come to think of it, he was not sure he wanted to marry Anuli either.

Seeing how Mbeku did not protest, Anuli spoke. "The things you mentioned, safety and strength, they aren't really about me. But you did win, so I will try to give you the things you want as a reward. I'm not sure how yet."

King Ibem spoke up. "I have a suggestion. I always need more advisers. If you agree, you will be safe here, that is, if Anuli agrees."

The lioness nodded. "Mbeku, what do you want?"

Mbeku thought quickly. He had been planning to argue that he won based on the literal words Anuli used, but now there seemed to be an opportunity for something else, something he had never even thought of before.

Mbeku addressed both of the lions. "Thank you, I accept your reward."

One of the animals started to cheer, and the others joined in. Soon the quiet land was taken over by celebratory noises, the loudest of which—a loud roar from King Ibem—quieted the crowd. Anuli shook her head at her father's antics and chose to move the conversation forward.

"Kalu," Anuli said, and turned to the leopard who was looking downcast. "I don't think you have to learn to lead to marry me."

"What?" Kalu stared at Anuli with wide eyes. "Marry you?"

"Yes. I want you to marry me." Anuli's relaxed tone was a clear contrast to Kalu's shocked state. "You can say no."

Kalu shook his head so fast that he blurred his vision. "No, I definitely do. Yes." He stopped talking, and his next words were hesitant, as if he were forcing them out. "Are you sure? If I'm not even going to help you out, there would not be a point in marrying me."

"You can join our hunters," Anuli said. "You can be something else entirely. Or you can just be you."

"Then... then if that's the case, I do want to marry you!"

With Kalu's approval, the competition ended with a marriage announcement. Next the leopards and the lions would have to meet and confirm the commitment between the two tribes. The tortoise settled into his role as adviser, and he enjoyed the safety it provided, but he never stayed for long in the lion kingdom before setting off on one journey or another. Usually, he'd come back being chased by mobs of animals that would stop at the boundaries of the lion kingdom.

Bonds that lasted lifetimes were forged that day of the competition, and when the animals returned to their homes, they told stories of the competition until it became a fable. The lessons were clear; that wisdom and trickery can sometimes be very similar and that family and love can be found in the most unlikely places.

CHAPTER 11
HOW DEATH CAME TO BE

In a time before the boundaries between body and spirit were as divided as they are now, a council of elders from communities across Igboland met to discuss a very serious matter: should humans die? The group of elders, titled members of the community, age-group leaders, and first-born children assembled in a large market center. Logs of felled wood were stacked in tiered rows held in place with woven raffia. The people took their seats and the murmur of voices increased to a steady rumble as more people arrived. Soon all the eight tiers were full, and the latecomers had to stand. The once-easy back-and-forth of voices took on a tense, hurried tone, and the energy of the crowd built to a crescendo.

Two men walked into the view of the assembled crowd, and the voices came to an abrupt halt. One of the men was slender and wore a simple red cloth tied across his body. His eyes, forehead, and feet were chalk-white from being covered in nzu. In his left hand he carried a divination bowl covered in raffia cloth. The other man wore a red, woven cap with an eagle's feather adorning the side. The top part of his face was scarred in thin lines placed diagonally across his face. He carried his ọfọ stick in his right hand, and on his body he wore a long white shirt over a red wrapper that cut off at his knees. Both men carried a distinct air of certainty and calm. The man with the feather, Ézè Anị, walked to the center of the crowd. As he moved, the cowry shells circling his wrists and ankles shook. Around his neck were strings of ivory beads. Each of his steps was accompanied by the gentle clink of shells. The dibìà, however, stilled his movements as he reached the crowd. The people next to him moved to make space, but he shook his head and stayed standing. Still, the space around him remained, and the dibìà stood apart from the crowd.

Ézè Anị cleared his throat as a woman walked up to him. In one hand she was holding a wooden plate filled with kola nuts. In another, she held a small bowl of palm wine. She was wearing a simple wrapper, and her hair, neck, wrists, and feet were adorned with ropes of red coral. She handed Ézè Anị the bowls and stood to his side. Ézè Anị looked out at the gathered crowd and seeing that he had their attention, he began the gathering by breaking kola. First, he thanked Chukwu, and then he thanked Anị for her bounty, Igwe for his rains, Amadiọha for his guidance and discipline, and Ìfèjiọkụ for her harvest. He made sure to include the alusị that he did not name directly as well. As he talked, he poured wine from a small calabash onto the ground. Next he thanked the gathered elders for their presence and asked for their wisdom in the meeting. He invited Chukwu, the alusị, spirits, and elders to partake in the kola. Finally he returned the palm wine gourd to Ézè Nwanyi, the woman next to him, and proceeded to break the kola into small lobes. He took a piece and passed the bowl to Ézè Nwanyi. She took her piece and carried the bowl around the ground. When everyone had been served, Ézè Anị started to speak.

"Our people."

The crowd focused their attention on Ézè Anị, who began to pace across the open space.

"Is it not said that the person who doesn't know where the rain started beating them won't know where it stops?"

The crowd murmured their assent, and affirmations bubbled through the crowd.

Ézè Anị continued. "Our elders have been unable to come to an agreement on an issue concerning the entirety of Igboland. And so you have asked me to consult Chukwu. You are gathered here now to listen to the message Chukwu has given ndi afa, his diviners. Is that not so?"

The assent of the crowd grew louder, and one man, wearing a red cap with a feathered end and leopard skin across his shoulders, spoke the loudest.

"Ise!" His booming voice startled a few people but drew chuckles from the majority of the crowd.

A wiry man standing next to him chuckled and clapped him on the back. "Ogbuagụ! The one that wrestles leopards. You always make your presence known, ehn?"

The man hailed as a leopard killer ducked his head. The action was a surprising contrast to his strong presence earlier, but no one seemed surprised. His actions provoked a good-natured round of chuckles and another friendly clap on the back from his neighbor.

Ézè Anị struck his stick on the ground, focusing the attention of the crowd once more. Then onye afa, the dibìà, stepped into the center of the crowd next to Ézè Anị and Ézè Nwanyi. The two moved to the side and gestured for him to speak.

"Our people, I bring a message. Do you want to hear it?" His voice was whispery thin, but it sounded clearly in the ears of the crowd.

Shouts of "yes," "we do," and "let us hear" poured out from the crowd.

The dibìà spoke. "I have connected to spirit to find the answers we seek. This is the message that was given to me." He paused. "There is to be a test."

The crowd quieted down and only sounds of soft breathing filled the air.

He continued. "Chukwu has heard our questions. He has heard that some of us are tired of this realm and wish to return to the world of spirits. They wish to introduce death to humans."

About half the crowd voiced their approval of this statement.

The dibìà continued over the sound of their approval. "And yet some of us do not wish to leave the realm of life."

This time, the other half of the crowd verbalized their assent.

The dibìà kept talking. "Chukwu has heard us, and so he has proposed a test. Each side will get a chance to choose an animal messenger: one carrying a message of death, another of life. Once we have chosen, Chukwu will send two messengers to us. The first one to arrive will determine our path going forward."

The crowd sank into silence as everyone digested the new information. Then the crowd split into two groups. After a moment of conferring, each group indicated that they had chosen an animal. The group in favor of life chose the dog to be their messenger. The dog was known to be a good tracker and a steady runner. The group wanting death chose the tortoise for his cunning. The journey between the spirit and the human realms was perilous, so they hoped the tortoise's trickster mind would give him an advantage. Once the messengers were chosen, the meeting came to a close. Ézè Anị was tasked with carrying the message of the people back to Chukwu.

That night, under Ọnwa's light, Ézè Anị sat on the earth in his outer courtyard with his eyes closed. His body was bare, save for a long white wrapper tied across his waist. His exposed skin was covered in white chalk. The only parts of his body that moved were his lips, but no sound came out. Ézè Anị sat in that courtyard until day replaced night. When Ézè Anị felt the warmth on his skin, he opened his eyes. After completing his morning rituals, a sacred time of contemplation and communion, Ézè Anị left for the day's meeting. Like the day before, the large market center was filled with people. The crowd came to attention once they spotted Ézè Anị. They were eager to hear the results of his labor.

Once again, Ézè Anị broke the kola and poured wine into the ground. He looked at the sea of faces staring back at him in rapt attention.

"Our people."

At the familiar greeting, the crowd spoke words of acknowledgment.

Ézè Anị continued the familiar role. Each time a meeting started, he had to confirm that his actions were in line with the desires of the people.

"I was asked to return to Chukwu with the messengers you have chosen. Is that not so?"

"It is so!" The crowd called out.

"I was asked to bring a message back from Chukwu regarding the outcome of the race. Is that not so?"

"That's right!" The crowd answered even louder. "We're ready to hear it."

Ézè Anị nodded at their calls and asked one last question. "Our people, do you want to hear the message I have for you?"

Once he received various forms of "yes," Ézè Anị shared the new message.

"Chukwu has sent the messengers. Last night I acted as an anchor between the worlds, and the animals have crossed into this realm. We will wait here. The first animal to reach us will have our answer."

Silence fell after Ézè Anị finished speaking. Then a woman with her hair wrapped in akwete cloth stood up to speak.

"Ézè Udo! Ézè Anị! I'm greeting you." The woman's voice came out like rustling leaves, one word moving sharply into the next.

Ézè Anị nodded his head toward the woman. "Adanma, we are lucky to have you here. What do you have to say? Please speak."

Adanma nodded and asked her question. "How will we know if we have the right messengers? Can't any random animal wander in?" The crowd chuckled, but no one disputed her question. They turned to Ézè Anị for an answer.

Instead, the dibìà raised his voice to answer. "I have opened my eyes to see what is unseen. I will know when the messengers come. To confirm it, I will ask it where it came from and what message it brings. When it responds, I will know for certain."

Satisfied, Adanma returned to her seat. None of the gathered crowd seemed to have any questions, and so the meeting ended much earlier than the last one. This time, though, no one went home. Community members who did not have a title—and therefore could not attend the meeting—arrived at the square carrying clay pots filled with food. Some contained rice or yams securely wrapped in banana leaves. Other pots contained various soups and stews. Some people brought bowls and other eating tools. Soon almost everyone present had a plate of food. Young children ran through the tight clusters of adults, chasing each other. The older youth sat in small groups and placed bets on what messenger would arrive first.

The people stayed outside until the bright light of day had settled into a warmer hue. The sky was dyed red from the disappearing light, but no one showed any signs of discontent or leaving. Most people had run out of energy, so they rested where they could. Now it was not just the older children sitting. Most of the people present formed groups and talked in low voices. The sound of moving feet attracted attention. The dibìà afa stood and walked toward the edge of the market. He squinted and peered into the distance.

"Something is coming."

The elders and titled people moved to stand with the dibìà, even though they could not see anything yet. Just as the last signs of light were disappearing, they spotted movement in the distance. The tortoise had arrived! He was moving so slowly that he looked like he was standing still, but the people watching could make out the clear outline of his shadow. They waited for the tortoise to get to them and stepped back to give Ézè Anị room to work.

The dibìà knelt to the ground and brought the tortoise to his eye level. He said something that no one could hear and then dropped his head to listen for a response. After a pause, he returned the tortoise to the ground. To the astonishment of the people, the tortoise faded out of existence, and some doubted that they had seen it at all. The onye afa stood and turned to face the people. He had a solemn look on his face that confirmed what the people had witnessed. The message was death.

The crowd felt that celebration would not be appropriate, so they dispersed. The next day they would meet one last time to organize the new ways of the people. Ézè Anị repeated his actions from the night before and sat in his courtyard until first night, covered in nzu. This time when the warmth hit his skin, he paused a moment longer before opening his eyes. He knew nothing would be the same again.

Ézè Anị began another walk to the meeting grounds, but this time he was met by a crowd of people led by the onye agwụ. Rather than wait for him, the people had come to bring him. Together they returned to the market center. Once everyone settled, Ézè Anị broke the kola and began the meeting.

"My people, I have a message for you. Do you want to hear it?"

Again the crown answered, "Tell us."

Ézè Anị agreed and began to tell the people what Chukwu had revealed to him during the night. From that day forth, humans would now move between the world of the spirit and the world of beings. When people died, they would become spirits. However, Chukwu also listened to the requests of those who did not want to stay as spirits. Spirit humans would get to reincarnate. The goddess Ani, who created the new souls and brought them into the world, would also receive old souls at the end of their journey and send them back again at the right time. If a person had served their community well enough, they would become ichie, or an honored ancestor, even as a spirit. These spirits would get to choose when or if they wanted to reincarnate, and would support their lineage from the spirit realm.

When he was finished talking, Ézè Anị hit his ọfọ on the ground and sealed the new ways. The elders at the meeting returned to their communities and passed the message on to their people and descendants. From that three-day-long meeting, every Igbo person learned of death and the laws that came with it.

CHAPTER 12
THE MYSTERIOUS MESSENGERS

In the early period of the Nrì kingdom, Ézè Ǹrì was faced with a crisis. His advisers, the odoloma, had come to him with a problem: the people were too successful.

Ézè Ǹrì welcomed the elders in his obi. He sat in the central topmost seat of the long hall, while the elders settled into the seats placed in rows along each side of him. After breaking kola, Ézè Ǹrì addressed the council.

"You say the people are too successful?"

"Yes," Ọzo Maduka answered first. "Well, it's not a problem, per se." He chuckled and said, "Ézè, our people are strong. Our harvests are plenty, and our homes keep multiplying."

Ézè Ǹrì leaned back into his chair. "I don't see the problem."

"Please, forget this storyteller," Ọzo Ebube interrupted. "The problem is not our people at all. But the people are hardworking. Everybody's competing to sell everything they have grown or created. It's not smooth."

"Hey, Ebube, settle down," Maduka responded. His words were stern but his tone was light. The smile on Ebube's face reinforced the friendly energy the two men shared.

"Okay, I understand better. What do you propose?" Ézè Ǹrì had an idea. Each community could collect their produce together and sell things routinely, but he wanted to hear the council's thoughts.

Maduka and Ebube shook their heads, and the rest of the council followed suit.

"Ézè, we don't know." Nzè Jachi chimed in. "This is something that affects all our families, so we believe the answer should come from you."

"Ooh, I hear you." Ézè Ǹrì nodded as he spoke to show his assent. "I will go back and ask for answers, and then I will let you know."

His advisers expressed their gratitude, and the council spent the rest of the time discussing the general welfare of the people. Once the elders left, Ézè Ǹrì retreated to his private rooms to speak with Chukwu.

He washed himself and then marked his body with white nzu before sitting cross-legged on the ground. He told Chukwu what the elders had told him. He explained his ideas and asked for answers. Ézè Ǹrì felt a deep resonance from within, so he knew he had been heard.

The next day, four strangers arrived at Ézè Ṅrì's obi. They wore long white robes that hid their bodies from view. Their faces were covered with wooden masks, colored white with chalk.

"Welcome. Is there anything we can provide?" Ézè Ṅrì tried again. He greeted them but received no response. Next he offered them a bowl of kola nuts, but the strangers did not move their heads to glance at the bowl. They made no sign that they saw Ézè Ṅrì at all. He paused to consider, and then he quickly clapped his hands and sent for one of his children, Onogu, to show the visitors a space to sleep. Once they left, he sent for one of his diviners.

"Ézè!" The diviner greeted Ézè Ṅrì warmly.

"Ekene." Ézè Ṅrì greeted him by his first name. "I want you to observe the visitors that came today. They are spirits."

"Of course, Ézè. Leave it to me." He slapped his palm on his chest in affirmation.

Once Ézè Ṅrì sent him off, Ekene headed out of the compound. He had a plan. He walked into the forest and came back at night with a basket. He returned to his room in Ézè Ṅrì's compound and got to work. Inside the basket was a rat. Ekene pulled out the squirmy creature, making sure to support it with both hands. He moved his head closer and whispered a few things to the animal before letting it down.

The rat licked its paws and then scurried out of the room. It headed to where the four strangers were sleeping. Its nose twitched and then it darted toward the sleeping mat in the center. He crawled over the feet of his chosen victim. Feeling the creature, the spirit in the middle sat up.

"Orie, what is it?" The spirit to his right spoke up with a voice heavy from sleep.

"I thought I felt something." Orie looked around but could not find anything suspicious. "Maybe I... Afo! Wake up. There is a rat crawling on you."

"Eke, Orie, what is going on? A rat?" Afo took a moment to register the words before springing up and waking the last spirit. "Nkwo, wake up, there is a rat."

The four spirits were awake now just in time for them to watch the rat run outside. They were upset at their sleep being disturbed, but they did not bother to chase after the rat. They chose to go to sleep instead.

Back in his hut, Ekene welcomed the rat with a smile. While it was gone, he cut up some raw plantains to feed it, and the rat ate without restraint. Once it was done, Ekene released it back into the forest.

The next morning, Ézè Ǹrì met the men in their room, carrying a bowl of kola nuts.

"Good morning," Ézè Ǹrì greeted the spirits. "Eke, Orie, Afo, Nkwo, I welcome you."

The men were stunned, and the disturbance of the last night started to make sense. As one, they stood and accepted the kola from Ézè Ǹrì.

The spirit called Eke spoke first. "Thank you for welcoming us. You found the right names. I am Eke, and the other three are Orie, Afo, and Nkwo, like you said. We have a message from Chukwu."

Ézè Ǹrì smiled at the confirmation that he had the right names. Then he led the spirits into his obi.

"What message do you have for me?"

The spirit Nkwo spoke next. "Chukwu has heard your questions, so we were sent to reveal ourselves to you. I am Nkwo, as you know. The four of us, Eke, Orie, Afo, and myself, govern the market days. With our presence in this land, your people can access our domains. From now on, you can mark your days with our names. Each day will govern different markets that will be held by each community."

The spirits continued to teach Ézè Ǹrì for four days. They told him of the four-day cycle, the bigger eight-day cycle, the monthly lunar cycle, and even festivals. They explained when things were meant to happen. When they left, Ézè Ǹrì summoned the council and repeated what the spirits had said.

"I want you to spread this to all of our people. This is how we will continue to count the days."

The council accomplished the task they were given. They spread the news through their communities and before long, everyone in Igboland knew of the market days and the four mysterious messengers.

CONCLUSION

I was lucky to be born to a family that understood the value of stories. My mother's name means "talk is greater." What's left unsaid in her name is war. For example, my name from my grandfather Obiageli means "they came to eat" but specifically the name is that I came to eat wealth. My mother was born in the aftermath of the Biafran war, which my family, people, and country were reeling from. Her name reflects my grandfather's approach to the war and the spirit he raised my mother in—the belief that conversation and stories were the ideal response to conflict. I grew up with my family telling me endless stories, because of my mother's influence, and I was happy for it.

I immigrated to America at twelve, an age when I was discovering who I was, and so much of that happened in a new and, to me, scary world. In America, stories became my refuge. It was hard not to internalize feeling different in a world where even my name—one of the most common Igbo names—was unique. I started to feel disconnected from myself, and almost unreal.

My stories became a reminder that there were worlds where I was real. Yet my elders, and the wisdom of their stories, could not prepare me for all of my journey. America was a new reality for me. My ancestors had created stories in a world where (as a people) our basic personhood wasn't in question. My insular childhood had preserved that narrative for me. Experience would teach me how I had always been impacted by anti-Blackness, but America was my first conscious contact with it. I shrank into myself further. I was scared.

I remember when I first heard the Audre Lorde quote "Your silence will not protect you." I thought she had written that just for me. That quote led me to read *Sister Outsider*. I felt less alone in my experience, because I wasn't. Soon after Lorde came Zora Neale Hurston's "If you are silent about your pain, they will kill you and say you enjoyed it" and Assata Shakur's "It is our duty to fight for our freedom." Then came music. Tracy Chapman, Gil Scott-Heron. People were gifting me stories too. My friends told me to read James Baldwin, Frantz Fanon, Toni Morrison. I sucked up every story I could like they were air. I needed them to live. I learned different stories; that there's not much difference between puff puff and beignets. There's okra in gumbo and both zobo and sorrell are made from hibiscus. From Nigeria to Georgia and Brazil to Jamaica, Haiti, and Cuba, there were songs and books, people and spirits that worked to voice the truth of the past and honor our collective Black futures.

All this and more led to how I wrote this book. For instance, Adaku's story takes place early in the fifteenth century. At this time, trade began to expand between precolonial Africa and Europe. Water spirits are a concept as old as Igbo people ourselves. Yet mermaids are a cultural and spiritual response to modernity. I attempted to capture the newness of Adaku's spirit, even as she continues in something older than she. The animal fables are where my family shows the loudest. As I wrote them, I was reminded of the voices and animated storytelling of my family, and they were with me again, even the ones not in this realm. If you have made it this far, thank you for honoring me and my stories.

GLOSSARY

Ada Ugo *(Ah-Dah Oo-Go)*—A term of endearment.

Afa *(Ah-FA)*—Divination, a method of consulting spirits.

Àfò *(Ah-fO)*—The third day in the four-day Igbo week.

Agwu *(Ah-GWU)*—The god-spirit that embodies health, medicine, and divination, and is considered to be the patron of dibìàs.

Ajo chi *(AH-Joh CH-IH)*—Bad chi. Used in reference to a personal spirit.

Ajo-m̀mụo *(Ah-JOH MM-woh)*—"Bad spirit," in reference to any spirit that has malicious or harmful intentions.

Ala Igbo *(Ah-la Ih-GBO)*—Igboland, the ancestral homeland of Igbo people, located in what is now southeastern Nigeria.

Alusị *(Ah-loo-see)*—A god/gods.

Amadịọha *(Ah-ma-di-OR-hA)*—God of justice, truth, love, and peace. He also represents the collective will of the people. He speaks in thunder and lightning. In some tribes, he is considered a spouse to Anị or, sometimes Anyanwụ.

Anị *(Ah-NEE)*/**Ana** *(Ah-NA)*/Ala *(Ah-LA)*—The earth; the god of the land, sometimes considered a spouse to Amadịọha.[3] Anyanwụ (Ah-nya-nwOO)—The sun god. Sometimes represented as a man, or a woman, or something else entirely. She is also considered a messenger to Chukwu.

Arò *(Ah-roh)*/**àkà** *(Ah-kah)*/**afo** *(Ah-fo)*—A year.

Chi *(Ch-IH)*—Spirit, either in reference to "ajo chi," a type of spirit, or "chi," the human spirit that holds a person's destiny.

Chineke bu m̀mụo *(ChIh-nak-E boo mm-woh)*—A common saying, meaning "the creator is a spirit."

Chukwu *(ChOO-kwOO)*—A name for the creator god, the great chi.

Dibìà *(Dee-Bi-Yah)*—A healer, priest, diviner, and spiritual leader.

Dibìà afa *(Dee-bi-yah-ah-FA)*—A dibìà that primarily divines.

Dù *(DU)*—is.

Egusi *(Ay-gwoo-see)*—Ground melon seeds. When cooked, they take on a bright-yellow color.

Egwu ọnwa *(Ay gwoo oh-nwah)*—Moonlight music that is played when communities gather at night to tell stories and exchange songs.

Èke *(AA-kay)*—The first day in the Igbo four-day week; also, the word for python.

3 Anị is "beneath"; Ana is "earth," and Ala is "land." But "Anị" is earth when it's the deity/realm, and in some communities, "Ala" is earth. In some communities these words may be used differently, but they all also mean the same thing.

Ekwensu *(Ay-kwain-sooh)*—The war god and a trickster god.

Ézè *(EH-ZEH)*—King or priest.

Ézè Ǹrì *(Eh-zeh N-rIH)*—The head priest of the Kingdom of Nrì, a spiritual position.

Idemili *(EE-de-mm-illi)*—A water spirit, and the name of a river in Igboland.

Ìfèjiọkụ *(Ee-fay-gee-oh-ku)*—The god of the yam harvest.

Igbo enwe ézè *(Ih-GBO Eh-nway Eh-Zeh)*—"Igbos do not have kings."

Igwe *(EE-gwAy)*—The sky; a title, sometimes referring to a spiritual title or a ruler; a deity.

Ikenga *(Ih-Ken-Ga)*—A physical representation, often carved from wood, of a person's willpower, strength, and fortune.

Ikwa ọjị *(Ih-kwa Or-gee)*—To break kola.

Ínú *(ee-Noo)/* **Ílú** *(Ih-Loo)*—Proverbs.

Iyi ùwà *(EE-yee OO-wa)*—An item that binds an ògbanje spirit to their current incarnation/life.

Izu *(EE-zOO)*—The Igbo four-day week.

Ji *(J-ee)*—Yam, a staple crop indigenous to Igbo people.

Kola *(Ko-la)*—A nut that grows in Igboland; symbolizes life.

Mbari *(Mm-ba-ree)*—A style of art where a house is constructed and then left to decompose naturally.

Mma *(Mm-ah)*—Good/goodness.

Ṁbala *(Mm-ba-lah)*—Compound, or a large area housing a family.

Ṁgba *(Mm-gba)*—Wrestle.

Ṁmadù *(Mm-ah-doo)*—Person/human.

Ṁmụo *(Mm-wooh)*—Spirit.

Ṁmụo mmili *(Mm-woh Mm-Ih-lih)*—Water spirit.

Ṅchòlòkòtò *(N-chor-lor-kor-tor)*, **nchò** *(N-cho)*, or **ịchò** *(Ih-cho)*—A traditional game played with stone or pebble pieces and a wooden board. Can also be played in the ground, with a makeshift board.

Ndù *(N-doo)*—Life.

Nkwo *(N-kwoh)*—The fourth day in the Igbo week.

Nnà *(N-NA)*—Father.

Nné *(N-NAY)*—Mother.

Nrì *(N-REE)*—One of the oldest Igbo kingdoms; some consider it to be the first.

Nsọ *(N-suh)*—Taboo, abomination, sacrilege.

Nzè *(N-zeh)*—A title.

Òbi *(Oh-bEE)*/ **òbu** *(Oh-bOO)*—The meeting room for the head of a compound.

Obi *(Oh-bee)*—heart. Can also be a name.

Òbi *(Oh-bee)*—A ruler's title.

Obi-Ukwu *(Oh-bee Oo-koo)*—Chukwu's court. Also, a large meeting room. Larger than a standard Obi, and usually belonging to a very high ranking person.

Ògbanje *(Oh-Gba-NjaY)*—A repeating spirit.

Ọha *(Aw-HA)*—The leaves of a native tree, used in soups and other dishes.

Okro *(Aw-Kraw)*/**Okra** *(Aw-kra)*—A crop native to West Africa; used in numerous soups and dishes.

Òmenàànì *(Oh-may-na-nee)*—The laws of Igboland.

Ọmụ *(Orh-MOO)*—A title.

Ọnwa *(Orh-N-waA)*—The moon.

Onwa *(Ohn-waA)*—A month.

Onye afa *(Oh-NYAY ah-FA)*—A diviner.

Onye kwe, chi ya ekwe *(OhN-YAY-KWAY Ch-ih YA ay-kway)*—If a person agrees (to something), so does their chi.

Ọ̀ràézè Ǹrì *(Oh-Ra-Eh-Zeh NRee)*—The Kingdom of Nrì.

Oyè *(Oh-RYE)*–The second day in the Igbo four-day week.

Ọzo *(Orh-Zoh)*—A title, usually given to elders.

Ụbòsì *(Uu-Boh-See)*/**Ụbọchị** *(Uu-Boh-ChIh)*—A day.

Ùlì *(Oo-Lee)*/**Ùshe** *(Oo-Shay)*—Decorative and spiritual patterns used on bodies, architecture, and clothing.

UmuNrì *(Oo-Moo NRee)*—The children of Ǹrì.

Ụwà *(Uu-WaA)*—The world.

RECOMMENDED BOOKS

Ikenga, by Nnedi Okorafor

The Girl With the Magic Hands, by Nnedi Okorafor

Wise Tales: A Collection of Nigerian Folktales, by Titilope Akinleye-Alinmo

What Happened to Waka Dimpolo, by Chidi Paige

The Big Ceremony, by Ozi Okaro

Feyi Fay series, by Simisayo Brownstone

Zeze the Copycat: A Heartwarming Rhyming Book for Kids about Being Yourself and Individuality, by Oye Akintan

The Unstoppable Three: Ridiculous Risky Revenge, by Sharon Abimbola Salu

ACKNOWLEDGMENTS

To ATony, Cora, Sadies, Qiana, and Delaney.

To my editor Renee, for helping shape this book into what it is now, and for guiding a very nervous debut author through this terrifying process.

For every space that has given me breath, every arm that has held me, and every kitchen that fed me—thank you.

ABOUT THE AUTHOR

Chinelo Anyadiegwu is a writer and graduate student. When they aren't writing stories about fantasy realms or mythology, they are writing grants. In their free time, they play video games of all sorts, from Tabletops and MMOs to Sandbox RPGs.

Printed in the USA
CPSIA information can be obtained
at www.ICGtesting.com
CBHW050846210424
7177CB00011B/234